GREAT TASTES

ONE POT

First published in 2010 by Bay Books, an imprint of Murdoch Books Pty Limited
This edition published in 2010.

Murdoch Books Australia
Pier 8/9
23 Hickson Road
Millers Point NSW 2000
Phone: +61 (0) 2 8220 2000
Fax: +61 (0) 2 8220 2558
www.murdochbooks.com.au

Murdoch Books UK Limited
Erico House, 6th Floor
93–99 Upper Richmond Road
Putney, London SW15 2TG
Phone: +44 (0) 20 8785 5995
Fax: +44 (0) 20 8785 5985
www.murdochbooks.co.uk

Chief Executive: Juliet Rogers
Publishing Director: Kay Scarlett
Publisher: Lynn Lewis
Senior Designer: Heather Menzies
Designer: Lena Lowe
Production: Kita George

ISBN: 9780681690875

PRINTED IN CHINA

OVEN GUIDE: You may find cooking times vary depending on the oven you are using. For fan-forced ovens, as a general rule, set the oven temperature to 20°C (35°F) lower than indicated in the recipe.

GREAT TASTES

ONE POT

More than 120 easy recipes for every day

bay books

CONTENTS

ONE-POT BASICS

There are no complicated tricks to making wonderful one-pot dishes, be they stews, soups, tagines or casseroles. There are no fancy techniques to master or last-minute difficult finishes to pull off. What could be better? What you get for relatively little effort is a kitchen filled with delicious aromas and a tender, flavoursome meal that will satisfy the whole family... all from one pot. It's easy on the washing-up, too.

The most important aspect of a one-pot meal is the process of long, slow cooking which results in a tender, flavoursome dish. Whether this is achieved in an oven or on top of a stove, in a casserole dish, a saucepan or a tagine doesn't matter.

Fish and poultry, meat and pulses, vegetables and even fruit can all be incorporated into one-pot dishes. Once you have mastered the basics, you'll quickly realise that most one-pots, from the humblest to the more exotic, are put together along similar lines. The differences lie in the ingredients and embellishments.

We are all a little bit envious of those confident cooks who can (seemingly) just throw a few ingredients into a pot and magically produce a richly fragrant sauce packed with tender meat and vegetables. But once you've gained confidence with the preparation methods, you'll find that it's easy to improvise and to adapt the recipes in this book to suit your own tastes. For example, many soups are blended in a food processor, but you may like to introduce more texture by leaving some of the soup unpuréed and mixing the two textures together..

Cheap cuts

You may be using the freshest ingredients you can find but they certainly don't need to be the most expensive when it comes to one-pots. One of their great advantages is that they are generally better if made with the more economical cuts of meat. Unlike expensive cuts, which are usually cooked quickly, the cheaper cuts are best when slowly simmered in liquid, a process which tenderizes the meat. You can tell when the meat is cooked because the pieces will break up easily with a fork.

Beef and lamb

Beef cuts such as blade, chuck, round or topside steak are ideal and generally have more flavour than fillet or rump and are less expensive. Lamb cuts such as neck chops and veal or lamb shanks are perfect and easy on the budget, too. Trim away any excess fat and sinew because they will toughen during cooking and can cause the meat to shrink.

Poultry and game

Chicken, turkey, rabbit and duck are all suitable for casseroling. Even when larger old birds are used, they are transformed into a tasty, tender meal. Any cut is suitable, although the breast, which

is more expensive and delicate, is better used with other cooking methods. Make sure the poultry or game is simmered gently, not boiled, otherwise the meat will toughen.

Whole chicken, chicken pieces, thighs, drumsticks and wings are readily available from chicken shops and some butchers. You'll find duck and turkey in some chicken shops and shops that specialize in game. In the freezer section of supermarkets you will find turkey in pieces (such as turkey breast roll), which are convenient to use.

Whatever type of meat or poultry you use, cut it into even-sized cubes. The size of the cubes depends on the type of meat and on the dish but somewhere between 2–3 cm (¾–1¼ inch) is the most usual. If the cubes are too small, the meat will fall apart into shreds during cooking.

Seafood

Seafood is high in protein and offers a wide variety of flavours and textures with the use of different types of fish, crustaceans and molluscs. Seafood is easy to prepare and does not take as long to cook as meat and poultry. The secret of a moist, tender fish casserole is to ensure it is not overcooked and the cooking temperature is low. Otherwise, it will become tough and dry. For fish and seafood casseroles, the sauce is often prepared first and fish added later.

Vegetables

Vegetables are highly nutritious and make an economical meal. Some vegetable dishes are more suitable for serving on the side with a main course or as a first course. Slow-cooking vegetables like potatoes, parsnips, turnips or sweet potatoes are an ideal addition to meat and poultry casseroles. Not only do they add flavour but will help thicken the sauce. The faster-cooking vegetables such as snow peas (mangetout), broccoli or mushrooms are usually added towards the end of cooking time to prevent them becoming too soft.

Legumes and pulses

Legumes and pulses are high in protein and fibre and add variety to your cooking. Some need overnight soaking to make them soft and cut down cooking time. If you are in a hurry, place the pulses in a saucepan, cover well with hot water and bring to the boil. Simmer for a couple of minutes, skimming froth from the top. Remove from heat and allow to soak for approximately one hour. After draining, they will be ready for use.

Those little extras

For really mouthwatering results, always select the freshest ingredients available. This could simply mean grinding up your own peppercorns or grating whole nutmeg if you have the time, rather than using ready-ground packet spices.

Some more exotic ingredients need not be expensive, especially when in season, and any effort spent in shopping or preparation will be well rewarded with enhanced flavour.

Stock

A well-prepared stock is the foundation of many a great stew, soup or casserole. Making your own isn't difficult. Beef, veal and chicken are excellent to use as a base.

Buy some beef bones (or whatever your chosen meat is) and ask your butcher to chop them into suitably sized pieces. Put them in a baking dish and bake for 30 minutes at 210°C (415°F/ Gas 6–7), turning occasionally. Alternatively, brown the bones in a little oil in a pan. Transfer the bones to a large saucepan and add chopped raw vegetables such as carrots, celery and onion. Cover with water, add seasonings such as whole peppercorns and a bouquet garni made of fresh herbs (such as a bay leaf and sprigs of thyme and parsley, tied into a bunch). Garlic may also be used sparingly. Too much can overpower the stock. Simmer stock gently, uncovered, for up to 2 hours, being careful not to let it boil. Strain, allow to cool and then store.

If making chicken stock, the back and neck can be used or the whole bird simmered, the liquid kept and the meat used separately. Or, if you have had a roast chicken for dinner, use the whole carcase.

Fish stock is easy to make using fish trimmings, herbs, water and a dash of white wine. It needs only a short amount of simmering time (about 30 minutes) because the taste will become bitter if it is left for longer.

Leftover fresh stock can be frozen for future use. Freeze in 250 ml (9 fl oz/1 cup) quantities in plastic bags.

Supermarkets sell a wide variety of stocks, in both dry and liquid form, which can be used instead of freshly made stock. Some commercial stocks are quite salty so if using them, don't add salt to the recipe until you have tasted the food..

Coating and browning meat

Once the meat or chicken is trimmed and cut ready for cooking, it should be coated in seasoned flour and browned on all sides in oil or butter. This will give the meat a crisp brown coating and a delicious taste. The flour also helps to thicken the liquid; usually, once you have coated the meat in flour you will not need to use another thickener at the end of cooking.

To coat the meat in flour, spread the flour on baking paper, sprinkle with a little salt and pepper and then turn the meat in the flour with your fingers or a pair of tongs. A less messy method is to put seasoned flour in a bag, add the meat cubes in batches, shake and then pick out the meat, shaking off any excess flour.

Instead of using salt and pepper for seasoning the flour, you could use paprika, celery salt, chilli or even stock powder, or whatever is appropriate to the flavour of the dish you're cooking. Don't sprinkle salt directly onto raw meat before cooking as it draws out the moisture and can make the meat tough and dry.

Don't coat the meat until you are ready to start cooking, as the moisture in it will absorb the flour and create a thick, gluggy coating on it, affecting the whole dish. Also, thoroughly shake off any excess flour from the meat before browning.

Browning meat also seals in the juices and gives a good rich colour to the finished stew. Brown meat quickly over a fairly high heat and turn it often to prevent it sticking and to brown it on all sides. Butter burns at a lower temperature than oil, but has more flavour, so use a blend of the two for browning.

Don't overcrowd the pan: the meat will stew in its juices and toughen if you do. Brown the meat in batches, if necessary.

Seasoning

When making both soups and stews, it is best to add seasoning at the end of the cooking process. Often, the liquid in the recipe has been reduced during simmering, making the flavours more concentrated; hence less seasoning is needed. Chilled soups should be tasted after chilling and may need more seasoning than hot soups. Some dishes thicken if left to stand and may need to have water or stock added to bring them back to the correct consistency—don't forget to taste for seasoning again if you have added more liquid.

Simmering

Generally, when making soups or stews, the ingredients are browned, liquid is added and the ingredients are then brought to the boil. The heat is then reduced and the pan covered and its contents left to simmer slowly until the ingredients are tender. Fish soups and stews are different in that the sauce is often prepared first and the fish added later to ensure it is not overcooked and becomes tough or dry. Fast-cooking vegetables, such as snow peas (mangetout), broccoli or mushrooms, are also usually added towards the end of cooking to prevent them becoming too soft and breaking up.

Soups and stews should never be boiled for long periods, or the meat will become tough and stringy and lose its flavour and any vegetables will break up completely. A dish is boiling when large bubbles appear in quick succession on the surface. A lazy simmer is best—tiny bubbles will appear at a slower pace on the surface of the food.

By the time a stew is cooked, there is quite likely to be a thin layer of fat on the surface which you can easily skim off with a spoon or some paper towels to make the dish healthier. If you are refrigerating the dish overnight, the fat will set and can be simply lifted off.

Thickening agents

If you find at the end of cooking that you need to thicken the soup or stew a little more, remove the meat and reduce the liquid by fast simmering for a short while, uncovered.

Another way to thicken a stew, rather than flouring the meat first, is to brown the meat, remove it from the pan and stir flour into the pan juices until well browned. Adding liquid will then create a sauce which is poured over the meat.

Cornflour or a slurry (a thin paste of flour and water) can also be added to the stew as a thickener towards the end of cooking. Another option is to use a beurre manié—a paste made of equal quantities of butter and flour, whisked into the sauce once the vegetables and meat are removed. If using a slurry or a beurre manié, boil the sauce for a few minutes to cook the flour.

Storing and freezing.

For busy cooks, a great advantage of soups and stews is that both methods lend themselves to cooking in batches and storing for later use.

Fish soups and stews and any delicately spiced Asian soups should be eaten as soon as they are cooked as their textures and flavours are impaired on reheating. But most meat dishes, especially those which are highly spiced, benefit from being refrigerated for a day or two before serving. This allows the flavours to mature and also gives you the opportunity to easily lift off any fat which may have formed on the surface of the dish. When you are ready to eat the stew, reheat it gently over a low heat, or microwave it on Medium-high (70%).

Many stews and some soups can be successfully frozen for 1 to 3 months. If you are making extra quantities with the idea of freezing leftovers, remember that potatoes don't freeze well, and cream curdles on reheating. So if the stew has potatoes or dumplings, or is finished with cream before serving, leave out these ingredients, and instead add them when reheating.

The food should be frozen as soon as it has cooled—and it should be cooled as quickly as possible to prevent bacteria forming. Skim any fat from the surface before you freeze a soup or stew.

The easiest way to freeze it is to put a plastic bag inside a jug or bowl, spoon the food into it, tie loosely and then put the jug or bowl in the freezer. When the food has frozen, remove the bag from the container, squeeze out as much air as possible and seal securely. Label and date it before returning it to the freezer. If you are cooking in bulk, it may be sensible to divide it into portions that can be thawed as single serves.

It is always best to thaw food completely in the refrigerator overnight before reheating. If you are reheating it in a ceramic dish, place the dish in the oven while the oven is still cold, then bring the oven to moderate (180°C/350°F/Gas 4) to prevent the dish cracking.

Some stews make great fillings for pies. Choose a stew that has no bones, or cut the meat off the bones. (If the sauce is too thin for a gravy, thicken it with a thickener described before.) Spoon the cold filling into a pre-baked pastry case, top with a pastry lid and bake in a moderately hot oven (190°C/375°F/Gas 5) for 30–40 minutes, or until heated through and golden brown.

Pans

When choosing a pan for making soups and stews, buy one that can be taken straight from the freezer to the stove or oven. A pan with a heavy base ensures an even distribution of heat which is important when dishes are simmering in liquid for a long time. A tight-fitting lid is essential to retain the moisture in the food.

Casserole dishes

When choosing a casserole dish, buy one that can be taken straight from freezer to oven or microwave. A tight-fitting lid is essential to ensure moisture is retained. The size of the dish is important. If it's too small, the liquid might overflow. If it's too large, the food will dry out because the liquid will reduce too quickly. The food should come approximately three-quarters of the way up the dish for the best result.

If the dish becomes stained during cooking it is best to allow it to cool and then soak it overnight in cold water. This will make most stains easy to remove.

Slow cookers

Slow cookers are a time-saving kitchen appliance that no busy household should be without. You prepare the ingredients, add the liquid, flick on the switch and leave the slow cooker to slowly simmer away, producing a meal of melting tenderness. Slow cookers use less electricity than an oven and there is no need to hover over them, stirring and fussing. They really do take care of themselves, capturing every drop of the food's natural flavour.

Tagines

Cooking in a tagine has become an attractive option, with the interest in Moroccan cooking on the rise. Tagines are now available in good cookware shops. Berber in origin, the tagine slaoui is a shallow glazed earthenware cooking pot that sits on a majmar, a charcoal brazier of unglazed earthenware. It has a conical lid with the top fashioned into a knob so that it can be removed easily with one hand when the simmering food has to be checked. Steam condenses inside the lid, falling back into the simmering food. The food cooked in these pots is called a tagine, or Moroccan stew. In modern Moroccan city kitchens, the food is often cooked in a saucepan or pressure cooker, then served in the tagine, especially if it is fully decorated and glazed.

The shallowness of the base is deliberate, so that the food may be accessed easily when eating with the thumb and first two fingers of the right hand in the Moroccan manner.

Before using, a tagine must be seasoned or 'matured', otherwise it could crack when first used. This also serves to remove the earthenware flavour, especially of the unglazed interior of the lid. While this is traditionally done on a charcoal brazier, an oven is the better option. Check that the tagine fits in the oven, removing the upper shelves. Preheat the oven to 150°C (300°C/Gas 2). Wash the new tagine and lid, and wipe dry. To the tagine base, add one peeled, roughly chopped onion, 2 roughly chopped carrots, 2 whole garlic cloves, 1 bay leaf and 2–3 tablespoons olive oil. Almost fill with water. Cover and place in the preheated oven for 40 minutes. Remove and leave at room temperature to cool slowly. Discard contents. wash tagine in hot suds and dry thoroughly. When cooking in a tagine, it is better to use it over a medium-heat charcoal fire; if using a tagine on a gas fire or an electric hotplate, low heat and a good heat diffuser are recommended. However, tagines are excellent for oven cooking.

Saucepans

Enamelled casseroles

Electric slow cooker

Tagine

SOUPS

MINESTRONE

SERVES 6–8

250 g (9 oz/2¼ cups) dried borlotti (cranberry) beans

2 tablespoons oil

2 onions, chopped

2 garlic cloves, crushed

80 g (2¾ oz/½ cup) chopped bacon pieces

4 roma (plum) tomatoes, peeled and chopped

3 tablespoons chopped parsley

2.25 litres (79 fl oz/9 cups) beef stock

3 tablespoons red wine

1 carrot, peeled and chopped

1 swede (rutabaga), peeled and diced

2 potatoes, peeled and diced

3 tablespoons tomato paste (concentrated purée)

2 zucchini (courgettes), sliced

80 g (2¾ oz/½ cup) green peas, shelled

80 g (2¾ oz/½ cup) small macaroni

parmesan cheese and pesto, to serve

1 **Soak the borlotti beans** in water overnight and drain. Add to a pan of boiling water, simmer for 15 minutes and drain. Heat the oil in a large heavy-based pan and cook the onion, garlic and bacon pieces, stirring, until the onion is soft and the bacon is golden.

2 **Add the tomato**, parsley, borlotti beans, stock and red wine. Simmer, covered, over low heat for 2 hours. Add the carrot, swede, potato and tomato paste. Cover and simmer for 15–20 minutes.

3 **Add the zucchini**, peas and pasta. Cover and simmer for 10–15 minutes, or until the vegetables and macaroni are tender. Season to taste and serve topped with grated parmesan cheese and a little pesto.

AUTUMN GARDEN SOUP

SERVES 6

30 g (1 oz) butter

1 large leek, white part only, sliced

1 garlic clove, crushed

1 teaspoon grated ginger

2 parsnips, peeled and chopped

1 medium celeriac, peeled and chopped

2 large carrots, peeled and chopped

3 potatoes, peeled and chopped

2 turnips, peeled and chopped

1.25 litres (39 fl oz/4½ cups) vegetable stock

2 tablespoons chopped chives

1 **Melt the butter** in a large heavy-based pan and add the leek. Cook over low heat for 15 minutes until very soft and lightly golden.

2 **Add the garlic** and ginger and cook, stirring, for 1 minute further. Add the vegetables and stock to the pan and bring to the boil.

3 **Reduce the heat** to simmer, partially covered, for about 40 minutes until very soft. Stir in the chives and serve.

SCOTCH BROTH

SERVES 8–10

750 g (1 lb 10 oz) best neck of lamb
   chops or lamb shanks

250 g (9 oz) pearl barley or soup mix
   (see Note)

1 carrot, peeled and diced

1 turnip, peeled and diced

1 parsnip, peeled and diced

1 onion, finely chopped

1 small leek, white part only, thinly sliced

75 g (2½ oz/1 cup) finely chopped
   cabbage

30 g (1 oz/½ cup) chopped parsley

1 **Cut away any** excess fat from the meat; place the meat in a large heavy-based pan with 2.5 litres (187 fl oz/10 cups) water. Bring to the boil, reduce the heat and simmer, covered, for 1 hour. Skim any froth from the surface. Meanwhile, soak the barley or soup mix in a bowl of water for 1 hour.

2 **Add the carrot**, turnip, parsnip, onion and leek to the pan. Drain the barley or soup mix and add to the pan. Stir to combine, cover and simmer for 1½ hours. Stir in the cabbage 10 minutes before the end of cooking time. (Add more water, according to taste.)

3 **Remove the meat** from the pan. Cool before removing from the bones. Chop the meat finely and return to the soup. Add the parsley and season.

Note: Soup mix is a combination of pearl barley, split peas and lentils.

SERVES 4

500 g (1 lb 2 oz) lamb shoulder steaks
2 tablespoons olive oil
2 small onions, chopped
2 large garlic cloves, crushed
1½ teaspoons ground cumin
2 teaspoons paprika
1 bay leaf
2 tablespoons tomato paste (concentrated purée)
1 litre (35 fl oz/4 cups) beef stock
2 x 425 g (15 oz) tins chickpeas
800 g (1 lb 12 oz) tin chopped tomatoes
3 tablespoons finely chopped coriander (cilantro) leaves, plus extra, to serve
3 tablespoons finely chopped flat-leaf (Italian) parsley
flat bread, to serve

1 Trim the lamb steaks of excess fat and sinew. Cut the lamb into small chunks.

2 Heat the olive oil in a large heavy-based saucepan or stockpot, add the onion and garlic and cook over low heat for 5 minutes, or until the onion is soft. Add the meat, increase the heat to medium and stir until the meat changes colour.

3 Add the cumin, paprika and bay leaf to the pan and cook until fragrant. Add tomato paste and cook for about 2 minutes, stirring constantly. Add the beef stock to the pan, stir well and bring to the boil.

4 Drain the chickpeas, rinse them and add to the pan, along with the tomato and chopped coriander and parsley. Stir, then bring to the boil. Reduce heat and simmer for 2 hours, or until the meat is tender. Stir occasionally. Season to taste. Garnish with the extra coriander and serve with bread.

MEDITERRANEAN FISH SOUP

SERVES 6–8

1 kg (2 lb 4 oz) white fish fillets

3 tablespoons olive oil

2 large onions, chopped

1–2 garlic cloves, crushed

4 large tomatoes, peeled, seeded and chopped

2 tablespoons tomato paste (concentrated purée)

6 tablespoons chopped gherkins (pickles)

1 tablespoon chopped capers

1 tablespoon pitted and chopped green olives

1 tablespoon pitted and chopped black olives

750 ml (26 fl oz/3 cups) fish stock

250 ml (9 fl oz/1 cup) white wine

1 bay leaf

3 tablespoons chopped basil

60 g (2 oz/1 cup) chopped parsley

1 Remove the skin and bones from the fish and chop into bite-sized pieces. Heat the oil in a large heavy-based pan and cook the onion and garlic for 8 minutes until soft.

2 Stir in the tomato and tomato paste. Stir for 2–3 minutes, or until the tomato is soft. Stir in the gherkins and half the capers and olives.

3 Add the fish, stock, wine and bay leaf and season well. Bring mixture slowly to the boil, reduce the heat and simmer for 10–12 minutes, or until the fish is just cooked. Stir in the herbs. Add the remaining capers and olives. Serve.

Notes: This soup is not suitable for freezing. Use a variety of whatever white firm fish is available, but take care to remove all the bones.

CLAM CHOWDER

SERVES 4

1.5 kg (3 lb 5 oz) fresh clams (vongole) in shell

1 tablespoon oil

3 bacon slices, chopped

1 onion, chopped

1 garlic clove, crushed

4 potatoes, cubed

310 ml (10¾ fl oz/1¼ cups) fish stock

500 ml (17 oz/2 cups) milk

125 ml (4 fl oz/½ cup) cream

3 tablespoons chopped parsley

1 **Discard any clams** which are already open. Put the remainder in a large heavy-based pan with 250 ml (9 fl oz/ 1 cup) water. Simmer, covered, over low heat for 5 minutes, or until the shells open (discard any clams which do not open during cooking). Strain the liquid and reserve. Remove clam meat from the shells, discarding the shells.

2 **Heat the oil** in a clean pan and then add the bacon, onion and garlic. Cook, stirring, until the onion is soft and the bacon golden. Add the potato and stir to combine.

3 **Measure the reserved** clam liquid and add enough water to make it up to 310 ml (10¾ fl oz/1¼ cups). Add this to the pan with the stock and milk. Bring to the boil and then reduce the heat, cover and simmer for 20 minutes, or until the potato is tender.

4 **Uncover and leave** to simmer for a further 10 minutes, or until reduced and slightly thickened. Add the cream, clam meat, salt and pepper to taste and parsley. Heat through very gently before serving but do not allow to boil or the flavour will be impaired.

SPICY LAMB SOUP

SERVES 4–6

2 large onions, roughly chopped

3 red chillies, seeded, chopped (or 2 teaspoons dried chilli)

3–4 garlic cloves

2 cm (¾ inch) piece ginger, chopped

1 teaspoon ground black pepper

6 cm (2½ inch) piece lemon grass, white part only, chopped

½ teaspoon ground cardamom

2 teaspoons ground cumin

½ teaspoon ground cinnamon

1 teaspoon ground turmeric

2 tablespoons peanut oil

1.5 kg (3 lb 5 oz) lamb neck chops

2–3 tablespoons vindaloo paste (see Note)

580 ml (20¼ fl oz/2⅓ cups) coconut cream

3 tablespoons soft brown sugar

2–3 tablespoons lime juice

4 makrut (kaffir lime) leaves

coriander (cilantro) leaves, to serve

1 **Put the onion,** chilli, garlic, ginger, pepper, lemon grass and spices in a food processor. Process to a paste. Heat half the oil in a large pan and brown the chops in batches. Remove to a plate.

2 **Add the remaining** oil to the pan and cook the spice and vindaloo pastes for 2–3 minutes. Add the chops and 1.75 litres (61 fl oz/7 cups) water, cover and bring to the boil. Reduce the heat; simmer, covered, for 1 hour. Remove the chops from the pan and stir in the coconut cream. Remove the meat from the bones, shred and return to the pan.

3 **Add the sugar,** lime juice and leaves. Simmer, uncovered, over low heat for 20–25 minutes, until slightly thickened. Garnish with coriander.

Note: This soup is quite spicy even without the addition of the vindaloo curry paste. Vary the amount of paste added to reach the desired spiciness.

SERVES 6

1 eggplant (aubergine), chopped

1 tablespoon olive oil

1 large onion, chopped

1 large red capsicum (pepper), chopped

1 large green capsicum (pepper), chopped

2 garlic cloves, crushed

3 zucchini (courgettes), sliced

2 x 400 g (14 oz) tins crushed tomatoes

1 teaspoon dried oregano

½ teaspoon dried thyme

1 litre (35 fl oz/4 cups) vegetable stock

80 g (2¾ oz/½ cup) pasta spirals

shaved parmesan cheese, to serve

1   Place the eggplant in a colander and sprinkle generously with salt. Leave for 20 minutes, then rinse and pat dry with paper towels.

2   Heat the oil in a large pan and cook the onion for 10 minutes, until soft and lightly golden. Add the capsicum, garlic, zucchini and eggplant and cook for 5 minutes.

3   Add the tomato, herbs and stock. Bring to the boil, reduce heat and simmer for 10 minutes, until tender. Add pasta and cook for 15 minutes, until tender. Serve with parmesan cheese.

MULLIGATAWNY SOUP

SERVES 4

375 g (13 oz) boneless, skinless chicken thighs

2 tablespoons tomato chutney

1 tablespoon mild Indian curry paste

2 teaspoons lemon juice

½ teaspoon ground turmeric

1.25 litres (44 fl oz/5 cups) chicken stock

1 onion, finely chopped

1 all-purpose potato, diced

1 carrot, diced

1 celery stalk, diced

4 tablespoons basmati rice

2 tablespoons chopped coriander (cilantro) leaves

1 Prepare the chicken by trimming off any fat. Cut the chicken into small cubes.

2 Put the tomato chutney, curry paste, lemon juice and turmeric in a large non-stick pan and mix with some of the stock. Add the remaining stock. Add chicken, onion, potato, carrot, celery and rice. Cook over a low heat, covered, for about 45 minutes, or until the chicken, vegetables and rice are cooked.

3 Season to taste with salt and freshly ground black pepper. Ladle soup into bowls and garnish with the coriander.

SERVES 6

2 red capsicums (peppers)

1 long red chilli

2 tablespoons extra virgin olive oil

1 onion, finely chopped

1 tablespoon tomato paste
(concentrated purée)

2–3 teaspoons harissa, to taste
(see Note)

4 garlic cloves, finely chopped

2 teaspoons ground cumin

750 ml (26 fl oz/3 cups) fish stock

400 g (14 oz) tin crushed tomatoes

750 g (1 lb 10 oz) firm white fish, such
as blue eye cod or ling, cut into 2 cm
(¾ inch) cubes

2 bay leaves

2 tablespoons chopped coriander
(cilantro) leaves

1 Cut the capsicums into quarters and remove membrane and seeds. Cut the chilli in half and remove the seeds. Place the capsicum and chilli, skin side up, under a hot grill (broiler) and grill (broil) until the skin blackens. Remove and place in a plastic bag, tuck the end of the bag underneath and leave to steam until cool enough to handle. Remove the skin, cut the flesh into thin strips and reserve.

2 Heat the oil in a large saucepan and cook the onion for 5 minutes, or until softened. Stir in the tomato paste, harissa, garlic, cumin and 125 ml (4 fl oz/½ cup) water. Add the stock, tomato and 500 ml (17 fl oz/2 cups) water. Bring to the boil, then reduce the heat and add the fish and bay leaves. Simmer for 7–8 minutes.

3 Remove the fish and discard the bay leaves. When the soup has cooled slightly, add half the coriander and purée until smooth. Season with salt and pepper. Return the soup to the pan, add the fish, capsicum and chilli and simmer gently for 5 minutes. Garnish with the remaining coriander and serve hot with crusty bread.

Note: Harissa is a hot paste made from chillies which is used in North African cooking.

CHICKEN SOUP WITH COUSCOUS

SERVES 4

1.5 kg (3 lb 5 oz) chicken, quartered

2 tablespoons olive oil

2 onions, finely chopped

½ teaspoon ground cumin

½ teaspoon paprika

½ teaspoon harissa, or to taste (or
¼ teaspoon cayenne pepper)

2 tomatoes

1 tablespoon tomato paste
(concentrated purée)

1 teaspoon sugar

1 cinnamon stick

1 teaspoon salt

100 g (3½ oz/½ cup) couscous

2 tablespoons flat-leaf (Italian) parsley,
finely chopped

1 tablespoon finely chopped coriander
(cilantro) leaves

1 teaspoon dried mint

lemon wedges, to serve

1 **Remove and discard** the skin from the chicken. Heat the olive oil in a large saucepan or stockpot, add the chicken and cook over high heat for 2–3 minutes, stirring often. Reduce the heat to medium, add the onion and cook for 5 minutes, or until the onion has softened. Stir in the cumin, paprika and harissa or cayenne pepper. Add 1 litre (35 fl oz/4 cups) water and bring to the boil.

2 **Halve the tomatoes** horizontally and squeeze out the seeds. Coarsely grate the tomatoes over a plate down to the skin, discarding the skin. Add the grated tomato to the pot, along with the tomato paste, sugar, cinnamon stick, salt and some freshly ground black pepper. Bring to the boil, reduce the heat to low, then cover and simmer for 1 hour, or until the chicken is very tender.

3 **Remove the chicken** to a dish using a slotted spoon. When it is cool enough to handle, remove the bones and tear the chicken meat into strips. Return the chicken to the pot with an additional 500 ml (17 fl oz/2 cups) water and return to the boil. While it is boiling, gradually pour in the couscous, stirring constantly. Reduce the heat, then stir in the parsley, coriander and mint and simmer, uncovered, for 20 minutes. Adjust the seasoning and serve with lemon wedges to squeeze over, and crusty bread.

CHICKEN AND VEGETABLE SOUP

SERVES 6–8

1.5 kg (3 lb 5 oz) chicken
2 carrots, roughly chopped
2 celery stalks, roughly chopped
1 onion, quartered
4 parsley sprigs
2 bay leaves
2 teaspoons salt
4 black peppercorns
50 g (1¾ oz) butter
2 tablespoons plain (all-purpose) flour
2 potatoes, chopped
250 g (9 oz) butternut pumpkin (squash), chopped into bite-sized pieces
2 carrots, extra, cut into matchsticks
1 leek, white part only, cut into matchsticks
3 celery stalks, extra, cut into matchsticks
100 g (3½ oz) green beans, cut into short lengths or baby green beans, halved
200 g (7 oz) broccoli, cut into small florets
100 g (3½ oz) sugar snap peas, trimmed
50 g (1¾ oz) English spinach leaves, shredded
125 ml (4 fl oz/½ cup) cream
3 tablespoons chopped parsley

1 **To make the chicken stock,** place the chicken in a large pan with the carrot, celery, onion, parsley, bay leaves, salt and the peppercorns. Add 3 litres (105 fl oz/12 cups) of water. Bring to the boil, reduce the heat and simmer for 1 hour, skimming the surface as required. Allow to cool for at least 30 minutes. Strain and reserve the liquid.

2 **Remove the chicken** and allow to cool enough to handle. Discard the skin, then cut or pull the flesh from the bones and shred into small pieces. Set the chicken meat aside

3 **Heat butter** in a large pan over medium heat and, when foaming, add the flour. Cook, stirring, for 1 minute. Remove from the heat and gradually stir in the stock. Return to the heat and bring to the boil, stirring continuously.

4 **Add the potato,** pumpkin and extra carrot and simmer for 7 minutes. Add the leek, extra celery and beans and simmer for a further 5 minutes. Add the broccoli and sugar snap peas and cook for a further 3 minutes.

5 **Just before serving,** add the chicken, spinach, cream and chopped parsley. Reheat gently but do not allow the soup to boil. Keep stirring until the spinach has wilted. Season to taste with salt and freshly ground black pepper. Serve at once.

Notes: Do not overcook the vegetables; they should be tender yet crispy. The chicken stock (up to the end of Step 1) can be made 1 day ahead and kept, covered in the refrigerator. This can, in fact, be a healthy benefit—before reheating the stock, spoon off the fat which will have formed on the surface.

STEWS & CASSEROLES

MOROCCAN VEGETABLE STEW WITH MINTY COUSCOUS

SERVES 4

2 tablespoons olive oil
1 onion, finely chopped
3 garlic cloves, finely chopped
1 teaspoon ground ginger
1 teaspoon ground turmeric
2 teaspoons ground cumin
2 teaspoons ground cinnamon
½ teaspoon chilli flakes
400 g (14 oz) tin diced tomatoes
400 g (14 oz) tin chickpeas, rinsed and drained
80 g (3 oz/½ cup) sultanas (golden raisins)
400 g (14 oz) butternut pumpkin (squash), peeled and cut into 3 cm (1¼ inch) cubes
2 large zucchini (courgettes) (250 g/ 9 oz), cut into 2 cm (¾ inch) pieces
2 carrots, cut into 2 cm (¾ inch) pieces
185 g (6½ oz/1 cup) instant couscous
25 g (1 oz) butter
4 tablespoons chopped mint

1 Heat the olive oil in a large saucepan over medium heat. Add the onion and cook for 3–5 minutes, or until translucent but not brown. Add garlic, ginger, turmeric, cumin, cinnamon and chilli flakes, and cook for 1 minute. Add tomato, chickpeas, sultanas and 250 ml (9 fl oz/1 cup) water.

2 Bring to the boil, then reduce the heat and simmer, covered, for 20 minutes. Add the pumpkin, zucchini and carrot, and cook for a further 20 minutes, or until the vegetables are tender. Season with salt and black pepper.

3 Place the couscous in a large, heatproof bowl. Cover with 250 ml (9 fl oz/1 cup) boiling water and leave to stand for 5 minutes, or until all the water is absorbed. Fluff with a fork and stir in the butter and mint. Season with salt and ground black pepper, and serve with the stew.

PERSIAN CHICKEN

SERVES 6

1.5 kg (3 lb 5 oz) small chicken thighs

60 g (½ cup) plain (all-purpose) flour

2 tablespoons olive oil

1 large onion, chopped

2 garlic cloves, chopped

½ teaspoon ground cinnamon

4 ripe tomatoes, chopped

6 fresh dates, pitted and halved

2 tablespoons currants

500 ml (17 fl oz/2 cups) rich chicken stock

2 teaspoons finely grated lemon zest

80 g (3 oz/½ cup) almonds, toasted and roughly chopped

2 tablespoons chopped parsley

1 **Coat the chicken** pieces with flour and shake off any excess. Heat the oil in a large heavy-based pan over medium heat. Brown the chicken on all sides, turning regularly, and then remove from the pan. Drain any excess oil from the pan.

2 **Add the onion,** garlic and ground cinnamon to the pan and cook for 5 minutes, stirring regularly, until the onion is soft.

3 **Add the tomato,** dates, currants and stock. Bring to the boil, return the chicken to the pan, cover with sauce, lower the heat and simmer uncovered for 30 minutes. Add the lemon zest and season to taste. Bring back to the boil and boil for 5 minutes, or until thickened. Garnish with almonds and parsley and serve with buttered rice.

VEGETABLE STEW WITH COUSCOUS

SERVES 4

2 tablespoons olive oil

1 onion, sliced

2 teaspoons mustard seeds

2 teaspoons ground cumin

1 teaspoon paprika

1 garlic clove, crushed

2 teaspoons grated ginger

2 celery stalks, thickly sliced

2 small carrots, peeled and thickly sliced

2 small parsnips, peeled and cubed

300 g (10½ oz) pumpkin (winter squash), peeled and diced

2 zucchini (courgettes), sliced

375 ml (13 fl oz/1½ cups) vegetable stock

185 g (6½ oz/1 cup) instant couscous

30 g (1 oz) butter

1   Heat the oil in a large pan. Add the onion and cook over medium heat for 10 minutes, until very soft and lightly golden, stirring occasionally. Add the mustard seeds, spices, garlic and ginger and stir for 1 minute. Add the vegetables and stir to coat with spices.

2   Add the stock and bring to the boil. Reduce the heat and simmer, partially covered, for 30 minutes, until tender.

3   Put couscous in a heatproof bowl. Add 185 ml (6 fl oz/ ¾ cup) of boiling water and stand for 2 minutes. Add the butter and stir until melted, then fluff up the grains with a fork. Serve with the vegetables.

SERVES 4

8 lamb neck chops
4 thick bacon slices
30 g (1 oz) dripping or butter
1 kg (2 lb 4 oz) potatoes, sliced
3 carrots, sliced
3 onions, thickly sliced
500 ml (17 fl oz/2 cups) beef stock
4 thyme sprigs

1 Trim the chops, removing any excess fat, and cut bacon into short strips. Heat the dripping or butter in a pan and cook the chops until brown on both sides; remove from the pan. Add the bacon and cook until crisp. Remove from the pan and leave to drain on paper towels.

2 Arrange half the potato, carrot and onion in the base of a deep, heavy-based pan. Season with pepper and add half the bacon. Layer the chops over this and cover with the rest of the potato, carrot, onion and bacon.

3 Add the stock and thyme. Cover, bring to the boil, reduce heat and simmer for 1 hour, or until the lamb is very tender.

LAMB STEW

SERVES 4–6

4 tablespoons olive oil

1 kg (2 lb 4 oz) lamb shoulder, diced

1 large brown onion, finely chopped

4 garlic cloves, crushed

2 teaspoons sweet paprika

100 ml (3½ fl oz) lemon juice

2 tablespoons chopped flat-leaf (Italian) parsley

1 Heat the oil in a large, deep heavy-based frying pan over high heat. Cook the lamb in two batches for 5 minutes per batch, or until well browned. Remove the lamb from the pan.

2 Add the onion to the pan and cook for 5 minutes, or until soft and golden. Stir in the garlic and paprika. Cook for 1 minute. Return the lamb to the pan and add 4 tablespoons of the lemon juice and 1.75 litres (61 fl oz/7 cups) water. Bring to the boil, then reduce to a simmer and cook, stirring occasionally, for about 2 hours, or until the liquid has almost evaporated and the oil starts to reappear. Stir in the parsley and remaining lemon juice, season with salt and freshly ground black pepper, and serve.

BEEF AND RED WINE STEW

SERVES 4

1 kg (2 lb 4 oz) diced beef
3 tablespoons plain (all-purpose) flour, seasoned
1 tablespoon oil
150 g (5½ oz) bacon, diced
8 bulb spring onions (scallions), greens trimmed to 2 cm (¾ inch)
200 g (7 oz) button mushrooms
500 ml (17 fl oz/2 cups) red wine
2 tablespoons tomato paste (concentrated purée)
500 ml (17 fl oz/2 cups) beef stock
1 bouquet garni (see Note)

1   **Toss the beef** in the flour until evenly coated, shaking off any excess. Heat the oil in a large saucepan over high heat. Cook the beef in three batches for about 3 minutes each, or until well browned all over, adding a little extra oil as needed. Remove from the pan.

2   **Add the bacon** and cook for 2 minutes, or until browned. Remove with a slotted spoon and add to the beef. Add spring onions and mushrooms and cook for 5 minutes, or until the onions are browned. Remove.

3   **Slowly pour** the red wine into the pan, scraping up any sediment from the bottom with a wooden spoon. Stir in the tomato paste and stock. Add the bouquet garni and return the beef, bacon and any juices. Bring to the boil, then reduce the heat and simmer for 45 minutes, then return the spring onions and mushrooms to the pan. Cook for 1 hour, or until the meat is tender and the sauce is glossy. Serve with steamed new potatoes or mash.

Note: To make a bouquet garni, wrap the green part of a leek around a bay leaf, a sprig of thyme, a sprig of parsley and celery leaves, and tie with string. The combination of herbs can be varied according to taste.

CHINESE BEEF IN SOY

SERVES 4

700 g (1 lb 9 oz) chuck steak, trimmed and cut into 2 cm (¾ inch) cubes

4 tablespoons dark soy sauce

2 tablespoons honey

1 tablespoon rice vinegar

3 tablespoons oil

4 garlic cloves, chopped

8 spring onions, finely sliced

1 tablespoon finely grated ginger

2 star anise

½ teaspoon ground cloves

375 ml (13 fl oz/1½ cups) beef stock

125 ml (4 fl oz/½ cup) red wine

spring onions (scallions), extra, sliced, to garnish

1 Place the meat in a non-metallic dish. Combine the soy sauce, honey and vinegar in a small bowl, then pour over the meat. Cover with plastic wrap. Marinate for at least 2 hours, or preferably overnight. Drain, reserving the marinade, and pat the cubes dry.

2 Place 1 tablespoon of the oil in a saucepan and brown the meat in three batches, for 3–4 minutes per batch—add another tablespoon of oil, if necessary. Remove the meat. Add the rest of the oil and fry the garlic, spring onion, ginger, star anise and cloves for 1–2 minutes, or until fragrant.

3 Return all the meat to the pan, and add the reserved marinade, stock and wine. Bring the liquid to the boil, then reduce to a simmer and cook, covered, for 1¼ hours. Cook, uncovered, for a further 15 minutes, or until the sauce is syrupy and the meat is tender.

ASIAN-FLAVOURED BEEF STEW

SERVES 4

2 tablespoons olive oil

1 kg (2 lb 4 oz) chuck steak, cut into
  3 cm (1¼ inch) cubes

1 large red onion, thickly sliced

3 garlic cloves, crushed

3 tablespoons tomato paste
  (concentrated purée)

250 ml (9 fl oz/1 cup) red wine

500 ml (17 fl oz/2 cups) beef stock

2 bay leaves, crushed

3 x 1.5 cm (½ inch) strips orange zest

1 star anise

1 teaspoon Sichuan peppercorns

1 teaspoon chopped thyme

1 tablespoon chopped rosemary

3 tablespoons chopped coriander
  (cilantro) leaves

1   Heat 1 tablespoon oil in a large saucepan, add the beef and cook in batches over medium heat for 2 minutes, or until browned. Remove.

2   Heat the remaining oil, add the onion and garlic and cook for 5 minutes. Add the tomato paste, cook for 3 minutes, then stir in the wine and cook for 2 minutes.

3   Return the meat to the pan and add the stock, bay leaves, orange zest, star anise, Sichuan peppercorns, thyme and rosemary. Reduce the heat to low and simmer, covered, for 1½ hour–2 hours, or until tender. Remove the bay leaves and zest. Stir in 2½ tablespoons coriander and garnish with the remainder. Serve with rice.

BOUILLABAISSE

SERVES 6

ROUILLE

1 small red capsicum (pepper)

1 slice white bread, crusts removed

1 red chilli

2 garlic cloves

1 egg yolk

4 tablespoons olive oil

SOUP

18 mussels

1.5 kg (3 lb 5 oz) firm white fish fillets such as red mullet, bass, snapper, monkfish, rascasse, John Dory or eel, skin on

2 tablespoons oil

1 fennel bulb, thinly sliced

1 onion, chopped

750 g (1 lb 10 oz) ripe tomatoes

1.25 litres (44 fl oz/5 cups) fish stock or water

pinch of saffron threads

1 bouquet garni (see Note on page 31)

5 cm (2 inch) piece of orange zest

1 To make the rouille, preheat the grill (broiler). Cut the capsicum in half, remove the seeds and membrane. Place, skin side up, under the hot grill until the skin blackens and blisters. Leave to cool before peeling. Roughly chop the capsicum.

2 Soak the bread in 3 tablespoons water, then squeeze dry with your hands. Put the capsicum, chilli, bread, garlic and egg yolk in a mortar and pestle or food processor and pound or mix together. Gradually add the oil in a thin stream, pounding or mixing until the rouille is smooth and has the texture of thick mayonnaise. Cover and refrigerate until needed.

3 To make the soup, scrub the mussels and remove their beards. Discard any mussels that are already open and don't close when tapped on the work surface. Cut the fish into bite-sized pieces.

4 Heat the oil in a large saucepan and cook the fennel and onion over medium heat for 5 minutes, or until golden.

5 Score a cross in the top of each tomato. Plunge them into boiling water for 20 seconds, then drain and peel the skin away from the cross. Chop the tomatoes, discarding the cores. Add to the pan and cook for 3 minutes. Stir in the stock, saffron, bouquet garni and orange zest, bring to the boil and boil for 10 minutes. Remove the bouquet garni and either push the soup through a sieve or purée in a blender. Return to the cleaned pan, season well and bring back to the boil.

6 Reduce the heat to simmer and add the fish and mussels. Cook for 5 minutes or until the fish is tender and the mussels have opened. Throw out any mussels that haven't opened in this time. Serve the soup with rouille and bread. Or lift out the fish and mussels and serve separately.

CLAMS IN WHITE WINE

SERVES 4

1 kg (2 lb 4 oz) fresh clams (vongole) in the shell

2 tablespoons olive oil

1 small onion, finely chopped

2 garlic cloves, crushed

2 large ripe tomatoes, peeled, seeded and chopped

1 tablespoon chopped flat-leaf (Italian) parsley

pinch of freshly grated nutmeg

4 tablespoons dry white wine

1 **Soak the clams** in salted water for 2 hours to release any grit. Rinse under running water and discard any open clams.

2 **Heat oil** in a large flameproof casserole dish and cook the onion over low heat for 8 minutes, or until softened. Add the garlic and tomato and cook for 5 minutes. Stir in the parsley and nutmeg. Season with salt and pepper. Add 4 tablespoons of water.

3 **Add the clams** and cook, covered, over low heat for 5–8 minutes or until they open (discard any that do not open). Add the wine and cook for 3–4 minutes, or until the sauce thickens, gently moving the dish back and forth a few times, rather than stirring, so that the clams stay in the shells. Serve immediately, with bread.

BEEF CARBONNADE

SERVES 4

30 g (1 oz) butter

2–3 tablespoons oil

1 kg (2 lb 4 oz) lean beef rump or chuck steak, cubed

4 onions, chopped

1 garlic clove, crushed

1 teaspoon soft brown sugar

1 tablespoon plain (all-purpose) flour

500 ml (17 fl oz/2 cups) beer (bitter or stout)

2 bay leaves

4 thyme sprigs

CROUTONS

6–8 slices baguette

dijon mustard

1   **Preheat the oven** to 150°C (300°F/Gas 2). Melt the butter in a large sauté pan with a tablespoon of oil. Brown the meat in batches over high heat and then lift out onto a plate.

2   **Add another tablespoon** of oil to the pan and add the onion. Cook over medium heat for 10 minutes, then add the garlic and sugar and cook for a further 5 minutes, adding another tablespoon of oil, if necessary. Lift out the onion onto a second plate.

3   **Reduce the heat** to low and pour in any juices that have drained from the browned meat, then stir in the flour. Remove from the heat and stir in the beer, a little at a time (the beer will foam). Return to the heat and let mixture gently simmer and thicken. Season with salt and pepper.

4   **Layer the meat** and onion in a casserole dish, tucking the bay leaves and sprigs of thyme between the layers and seasoning with salt and black pepper as you go. Pour the liquid over the meat, cover with a lid and cook in the oven for 2½–3 hours, or until the meat is tender.

5   **To make the croutons,** preheat the grill (broiler). Lightly toast the baguette on both sides, then spread one side with mustard. Arrange on top of the carbonnade, mustard side up, and place the whole casserole under the grill for a minute.

HOISIN BEEF STEW

SERVES 6

1½ tablespoons peanut oil

1 kg (2 lb 4 oz) stewing beef (such as chuck), cut into 3 cm (1¼ inch) cubes

1 tablespoon finely chopped ginger

1 tablespoon finely chopped garlic

1 litre (35 fl oz/4 cups) good-quality beef stock

4 tablespoons Chinese rice wine

4 tablespoons hoisin sauce

5 cm (2 inch) piece cinnamon or cassia bark

1 piece dried tangerine peel

1 star anise

1 teaspoon Sichuan peppercorns, lightly crushed

2 teaspoons soft brown sugar

300 g (10½ oz) daikon, cut into 3 cm (1¼ inch) chunks

3 spring onions (scallions), cut into 3 cm (1¼ inch) lengths, plus extra, to garnish

50 g (1¾ oz) sliced bamboo shoots

a few drops sesame oil (optional)

1 **Heat a wok** until very hot, add the peanut oil and swirl to coat the side. Stir-fry the beef in four batches for 1–2 minutes for each batch, or until the meat is browned all over. Remove from the wok.

2 **Add the ginger** and garlic to the wok and stir-fry for a few seconds. Add stock, rice wine, hoisin sauce, cinnamon or cassia bark, tangerine peel, star anise, Sichuan peppercorns, sugar, daikon and 875 ml (30 fl oz/3½ cups) water, then return the beef to the wok.

3 **Bring to the boil**, skimming off any scum that forms on the surface, then reduce to a simmer and cook, stirring occasionally, for 1½ hours, or until the beef is tender and the sauce has thickened slightly. Add the spring onion and bamboo shoots 5 minutes before the end of the cooking time. Stir in a few drops of sesame oil, if desired, and garnish with extra spring onion. Serve with rice.

Note: You can remove the star anise, cinnamon and tangerine peel before serving or leave them in the dish for presentation.

ROMAN CHICKEN

SERVES 2–4

1 tablespoon olive oil

1 small onion, sliced

4 thick bacon slices, diced

4 large or 8 small chicken legs

1 garlic clove, crushed

4 tablespoons chopped parsley

250 ml (9 fl oz/1 cup) chicken stock

1 tablespoon chopped marjoram

440 g (15½ oz) tin crushed tomatoes

1   **Heat the oil** in a large heavy-based pan and cook the onion and bacon over medium heat for 5 minutes. Increase the heat and add the chicken in batches. Brown the chicken on all sides, turning often and taking care not to overcook the onion and bacon, for about 5 minutes.

2   **Reduce the heat**, add the garlic and parsley and cook for 2–3 minutes. Add the stock and marjoram, stirring well. Add the tomato, stir well and season to taste.

3   **Bring to the boil**, cover the pan and simmer gently for 30 minutes, turning the chicken legs occasionally, until they are cooked through.

CHICKEN IN SAFFRON STEW

SERVES 4

3 tablespoons olive oil

4 tablespoons blanched almonds

1 thick slice bread, crusts removed, cut into pieces

½ teaspoon ground cinnamon

pinch of saffron threads

2 garlic cloves

2 tablespoons chopped flat-leaf (Italian) parsley

1.5 kg (3 lb 5 oz) chicken, cut into 8 pieces and seasoned with salt

2 brown onions, finely chopped

125 ml (4 fl oz/½ cup) fino sherry

375 ml (13 fl oz/1½ cups) chicken stock

1 bay leaf

2 thyme sprigs

2 tablespoons lemon juice

2 egg yolks

1 Heat 1 tablespoon of the oil in a heavy-based flameproof casserole dish over a medium–high heat. Add the almonds and bread and fry for 3 minutes, or until golden. Remove and drain on paper towel. When cooled slightly, put in a mortar and pestle or food processor, add the cinnamon, saffron, garlic and half the parsley, and grind or process to a coarse, crumbly consistency.

2 Heat the rest of the oil in the casserole dish over medium heat and brown the chicken for about 5 minutes. Transfer to a plate. Add the onion and cook gently for about 5 minutes, or until softened.

3 Return the chicken pieces to the casserole dish with the sherry, stock, bay leaf and thyme and simmer, covered, over medium heat for 1 hour, or until the chicken is tender. Remove the chicken and cover to keep warm. Add the almond paste to the dish and cook for 1 minute. Remove from the heat and whisk in the lemon juice, egg yolks and remaining parsley. Return the casserole dish to the stovetop and stir over very low heat until just thickened slightly (do not allow it to boil or the sauce will separate). Season to taste, return the chicken to the casserole and gently warm through before serving.

CHICKEN IN SAMFAINA SAUCE

SERVES 4

1 kg (2 lb 4 oz) chicken, cut into
8 pieces

60 ml (2 fl oz/¼ cup) olive oil

2 large brown onions, chopped

400 g (14 oz) eggplant (aubergine),
cut into 2 cm (¾ inch) cubes

3 garlic cloves, crushed

350 g (12 oz) zucchini (courgettes),
cut into strips

2 green or red capsicums (peppers),
cut into 1 cm (½ inch) strips

2 x 400 g (14 oz) tins chopped tomatoes

1 bay leaf

2 tablespoons chopped herbs (such as
thyme, oregano and flat-leaf/Italian
parsley)

125 ml (4 fl oz/½ cup) white wine

1 **Season the chicken** pieces with salt and pepper. Heat the oil in a large heavy-based saucepan over medium heat, add the chicken in batches and brown well on all sides. Remove from the pan and reduce the heat to low–medium.

2 **Add the onion** and cook for about 10 minutes, or until softened. Add the eggplant, garlic, zucchini and capsicum and cook for 10 minutes, or until the vegetables are softened.

3 **Stir in the tomato,** bay leaf, herbs and wine, and return the chicken pieces to the pan. Bring to the boil, then cover and simmer over low heat for about 45 minutes, or until the chicken is tender and the eggplant is soft. Season well with salt and pepper before serving.

SERVES 4

250 g (9 oz/1¼ cups) dried white haricot beans (such as navy beans)

4 tablespoons olive oil

2 garlic cloves, chopped

2 brown onions, chopped

1 teaspoon sweet paprika)

1 teaspoon smoked paprika

2 teaspoons ground cumin

¼ teaspoon ground cinnamon

¼ teaspoon cayenne pepper

1 teaspoon dried rosemary

1 red capsicum (pepper), seeded and diced

750 g (1 lb 10 oz) pork tenderloin, roughly diced

400 g (14 oz) tin chopped tomatoes

250 ml (9 fl oz/1 cup) chicken stock

300 g (11 oz) orange sweet potato, peeled and roughly diced

60 g (2 oz) silverbeet (Swiss chard), washed well and shredded

1 Cover the beans with cold water and soak for at least 3 hours. Drain well. Preheat oven to 160°C (315°F/Gas 2–3). Heat 2 tablespoons of the oil in a large saucepan over medium heat, add half the garlic and half the onion and cook for about 5 minutes, or until soft. Add the beans and cover with water. Bring to the boil. Reduce the heat and simmer for 45 minutes, or until the beans are soft but not mushy.

2 Heat remaining oil in a large flameproof casserole dish over a medium heat. Add the remaining garlic and onion and cook for 5 minutes, or until softened. Stir in the spices, rosemary, capsicum and diced pork and cook until the pork is evenly pale brown. Add the tomato and stock, bring to the boil, then cover and cook in the oven for 1 hour. Add beans and sweet potato, top up with 250 ml (9 fl oz/1 cup) water and return to the oven for 30 minutes, or until the sweet potato is tender. Stir in the silverbeet and cook for 5 minutes, or until the silverbeet is wilted. Season to taste.

SPANISH PORK AND VEGETABLE STEW

SERVES 4–6

600 g (1 lb 5 oz) boneless pork shoulder (hand/collar butt)

4 (100 g/3½ oz each) all-purpose potatoes

1 red capsicum (pepper)

1 green capsicum (pepper)

2 tablespoons olive oil

1 large red onion, chopped

2 garlic cloves, crushed

100 g (3½ oz) jamón

1 chorizo sausage, sliced

2 x 400g (14 oz) tins tomatoes, chopped

10 g (¼ oz/½ bunch) thyme

2 tablespoons sherry vinegar

100 ml (3½ fl oz) white wine

1 bay leaf

250 ml (9 fl oz/1 cup) chicken stock

1 **Cut the pork** into 2 cm (¾ inch) pieces. Peel the potatoes and cut into same size. Seed and chop capsicums into 2 cm (¾ inch) squares.

2 **Preheat the oven** to 180°C (350°F/Gas 4). Place a large frying pan over medium heat. Heat the oil then add the pork, onion and garlic. Cook for 5 minutes until the onion is softened and the meat is lightly browned all over. Next add the capsicums, chorizo and jamón. Continue to cook, stirring occasionally, for another 5 minutes or until the liquid is slightly reduced.

3 **Place in a large**, deep ovenproof pan or casserole dish. Add the remaining ingredients and season with salt and pepper. Place in the oven and cook for 2 hours or until the meat is very tender.

Note: Jamón is a type of Spanish ham. Chorizo is a type of Spanish pork sausage containing smoked paprika. It's available fresh and also cured and smoked. Fresh ones must be cooked. Either type can be used in this recipe. Jamón and chorizo are available from delicatessens and some supermarkets.

SERVES 4

1 large onion, chopped

500 g (1 lb 2 oz) chuck steak, cubed

2 thyme sprigs, leaves only

1 tablespoon chopped parsley

2 bay leaves, crumbled

500 ml (17 fl oz/2 cups) good red wine

3 tablespoons brandy

2 tablespoons olive oil

50 g (1¾ oz) butter

6 bacon slices, chopped

12 small baby onions (or 6 French
   shallots), peeled

150 g (5½ oz) button mushrooms

2 garlic cloves, chopped

2 tablespoons plain (all-purpose) flour

375 ml (13 fl oz/1½ cups) beef stock

1 Put the onion, steak, herbs, wine and brandy in a bowl and stir well to combine. Cover with plastic wrap; refrigerate for 3 hours. Drain the meat, reserving all the marinade. Pat the meat dry with paper towels.

2 Heat 1 tablespoon oil and half the butter in a large heavy-based pan. Cook the bacon and baby onions, stirring regularly, over low heat until the onions are golden brown. Remove the onions and bacon from the pan with a slotted spoon and set aside on a plate or paper towels.

3 Add the mushrooms and garlic to the pan and cook, stirring, for about 2 minutes; lift them from the pan with a slotted spoon and set aside with the baby onions. Add the remaining oil and butter to the pan and when they are hot add the meat in batches and brown well. Return all the meat to the pan, sprinkle with flour and toss until all the pieces are well coated.

4 Add the reserved marinade to the pan with the stock. Bring to the boil, stir well, cover and simmer over a very low heat for 1½ hours, or until the meat is very tender. Put the browned baby onions, bacon and mushrooms back into the pan, season to taste and cook, uncovered, for 15 minutes. This is delicious with mashed potatoes.

HUNGARIAN VEAL GOULASH

SERVES 4

2 tablespoons olive oil

2 onions, chopped

500 g (1 lb 2 oz) stewing veal, cubed

1 tablespoon Hungarian paprika (see Note)

¼ teaspoon caraway seeds

425 g (15 oz) tin chopped tomatoes

500 ml (17 fl oz/2 cups) beef stock

1 large potato, diced

1 large carrot, sliced

1 green capsicum (pepper), chopped

125 g (4½ oz/½ cup) sour cream

1 **Heat the oil** in a large heavy-based pan. Fry the onion for 10 minutes, stirring often, until soft and golden brown. Remove the onion, increase the heat and brown the veal in batches. Return the veal and onion to the pan.

2 **Add the paprika**, caraway seeds, tomatoes and stock. Bring to the boil, reduce the heat, cover and simmer for 1¼ hours.

3 **Add the diced** potato, carrot and capsicum and cook, uncovered, until the vegetables are tender. Season to taste with salt and freshly ground black pepper, then stir in the sour cream. Serve with rice or pasta.

Note: Hungarian paprika, from good supermarkets and delicatessens, has a brighter colour and is not as sweet as ordinary paprika. .

COQ AU VIN

SERVES 6

plain (all-purpose) flour
2 kg (4 lb 8 oz) chicken pieces
3 tablespoons oil
4 thick bacon slices, sliced
12 small baby onions
2 garlic cloves, crushed
2 tablespoons brandy
375 ml (13 fl oz/1½ cups) good red wine
375 ml (13 fl oz/1½ cups) chicken stock
2 bay leaves
1 bouquet garni (see Note on page 31)
3 tablespoons tomato paste (concentrated purée)
250 g (9 oz) small button mushrooms

1 **Season the flour** with a little salt and pepper and coat the chicken; shake off any excess flour. Heat 2 tablespoons of the oil in a heavy-based pan and brown the chicken in small batches; drain on paper towels.

2 **Heat the remaining** oil in the cleaned pan. Add the bacon, onions and garlic and cook, stirring, until the onions are browned. Add the chicken, brandy, wine, stock, bay leaves, bouquet garni and tomato paste. Bring to the boil, reduce the heat and simmer, covered, for 30 minutes.

3 **Add the mushrooms**, stirring to combine, and simmer, uncovered, for 10 minutes, until the chicken is tender and the sauce has slightly thickened. Serve with crusty bread.

VEGETARIAN CHILLI

SERVES 6–8

130 g (4½ oz/¾ cup) burghul (cracked wheat)

2 tablespoons olive oil

1 large onion, finely chopped

2 garlic cloves, crushed

1 teaspoon chilli powder

2 teaspoons ground cumin

1 teaspoon cayenne pepper

½ teaspoon ground cinnamon

2 x 400 g (14 oz) tins crushed tomatoes

750 ml (126 fl oz/3 cups) vegetable stock

440 g (15½ oz) tin red kidney beans, rinsed and drained

2 x 300 g (10½ oz) tins chickpeas, rinsed and drained

310 g (11 oz) tin corn kernels, drained

2 tablespoons tomato paste (concentrated purée)

1 **Soak the burghul** in 250 ml (9 fl oz/1 cup) of hot water for 10 minutes. Heat the oil in a large heavy-based pan and cook the onion for 10 minutes, stirring often, until soft and golden.

2 **Add garlic**, chilli powder, cumin, cayenne and cinnamon and cook, stirring, for a further minute.

3 **Add the tomato**, stock and burghul. Bring to the boil and simmer for 10 minutes. Stir in the beans, chickpeas, corn and tomato paste and simmer for 20 minutes, stirring often. Serve with corn chips and sour cream.

PEPPERED VEGETABLE HOTPOT

SERVES 8–10

2 tablespoons olive oil

2 onions, chopped

2 leeks, white part only, washed and chopped

2 garlic cloves, crushed

1.5 litres (52 fl oz/6 cups) chicken stock

2 tablespoons chopped rosemary

1–2 teaspoons green peppercorns

4 large potatoes, cubed

2 large turnips, cubed

200 g (7 oz) broccoli, cut into small florets

200 g (7 oz) cauliflower, cut into small florets

155 g (5½ oz/1 cup) fresh or frozen peas

1 Heat the oil in a large heavy-based pan and cook onion and leek over medium heat for 10 minutes, or until tender.

2 Add the garlic and cook for 1 minute further, then add the stock, rosemary, peppercorns and potato to the pan. Bring to the boil and then reduce the heat, cover and leave to simmer for 30 minutes. Add the turnip and allow to simmer for a further 15 minutes.

3 Add broccoli, cauliflower and peas. Simmer, uncovered, for a further 5 minutes. Season with salt and freshly ground black pepper to taste.

Note: Serve as a main course with pesto and crusty bread.

OXTAIL RAGOUT

SERVES 4

1 kg (2 lb 4 oz) oxtail, cut into short pieces (ask your butcher to do this)

3 tablespoons plain (all-purpose) flour

1 tablespoon ghee or oil

2 bacon strips, chopped

1 small onion, peeled and studded with 6 whole cloves

2 garlic cloves

2 carrots, quartered lengthways

375 ml (13 fl oz/1½ cups) beef or chicken stock

425 g (15 oz) tin puréed tomato

1 parsnip, peeled and quartered lengthways

1 leek, white part only, thickly sliced

1 **Trim any fat** from the oxtail and discard. Put the oxtail in a large bowl, cover with water and set aside for 3 hours. Drain and transfer the meat to a large heavy-based pan, cover with fresh water and bring to the boil. Reduce the heat and simmer for 10 minutes, skimming any froth from the surface with a spoon or paper towel. Drain the meat, allow to cool and pat dry with paper towels.

2 **Preheat the oven** to 150°C (300°F/Gas 2). Put the flour and a little salt and pepper in a large plastic bag; put the oxtail in the bag and shake to coat with flour. Heat the ghee or oil in a large frying pan, add the bacon and cook over medium heat for 3 minutes, stirring frequently. Remove bacon from the pan.

3 **Add the oxtail** and cook, stirring continuously over a medium–high heat for 2–3 minutes, or until well browned. Transfer to a casserole dish.

4 **Add the bacon**, onion, garlic and half the carrot. Stir in the stock and tomato purée, then cover and bake for 3 hours. Add the remaining vegetables and cook for 30–40 minutes, or until tender.

HAM, BEAN AND SWEDE CASSEROLE

SERVES 4

200 g (7 oz/1 cup) black-eyed beans,
   soaked in cold water overnight

1 smoked ham hock

18 small baby onions

30 g (1 oz) butter

2 tablespoons oil

2 garlic cloves, crushed

2 tablespoons golden syrup or honey

3 teaspoons ground cumin

1 tablespoon German or French mustard

1 swede (rutabaga) or turnip, peeled
   and diced

2 tablespoons tomato paste
   (concentrated purée)

1 **Drain the beans** and place in a pan. Add the hock and 2 litres (70 fl oz/8 cups) water, cover and bring to the boil. Reduce to low; simmer for 30 minutes. Drain, reserving 500 ml (17 fl oz/2 cups) of stock. Remove the skin from the hock; chop the meat into bite-sized pieces.

2 **Peel the onions**, leaving the bases intact. Heat the butter, oil, garlic and syrup in the cleaned pan. Add the onions and cook for 5–10 minutes, or until just starting to turn golden.

3 **Stir in the ham**, cumin, mustard and swede or turnip and cook for 2 minutes until golden. Season and return the beans to the pan. Add the reserved stock and tomato paste, bring to the boil, reduce the heat and simmer, covered, for 1 hour. Uncover and simmer for 5–10 minutes longer, or until reduced and thickened.

Note: This stew can be made up to 3 days in advance. Store, tightly covered, in the refrigerator.

CAJUN SPICED FISH BRAISE

SERVES 4

750 g (1 lb 10 oz) ling fillets

2 tablespoons plain (all-purpose) flour

2 tablespoons Cajun spice mix

2 tablespoons olive oil

30 g (1 oz) butter

1 large onion, thickly sliced

1 red capsicum (pepper), sliced

125 ml (4 fl oz/½ cup) white wine

500 g (1 lb 2 oz/2 cups) bottled tomato
  pasta sauce

1 wide strip lemon zest

8 fresh raw prawns (shrimp), peeled
  and deveined

1 Cut the fish into bite-sized, thick pieces. Combine the flour and Cajun spice mix, then lightly coat the fish. Heat the oil and butter in a large heavy-based pan over medium heat. Cook the fish, turning occasionally, until browned on all sides. Remove from the pan.

2 Add the onion and capsicum to the pan and cook, stirring occasionally, for 5 minutes. Add wine and bring to the boil, stirring continuously. Add the tomato pasta sauce and lemon zest. Bring to the boil, then reduce the heat and simmer for a further 10 minutes.

3 Add the fish and prawns; cook over low heat for about 3 minutes, or until the prawns are red and the fish tender and easily flaked with a fork. Remove the zest and season. Serve immediately.

MINTY LAMB SHANKS

SERVES 6

6 lamb shanks
1 tablespoon olive oil
1 red onion, finely chopped
2 garlic cloves, crushed
35 g (1¼ oz/¾ cup) chopped mint
1 thyme sprig
2 bay leaves
425 g (15 oz) tin crushed tomatoes
500 ml (17 fl oz/2 cups) vegetable stock
3 tablespoons white wine

1 Preheat the oven to 200°C (400°F/Gas 6). Put the shanks in a baking dish in a single layer, close together. Season well. Bake for 20 minutes; turn the shanks, reduce heat to 180°C (350°F/Gas 4) and bake for 20 minutes.

2 Heat the oil in a frying pan. Cook the onion and garlic for 5–8 minutes, or until soft. Stir in 25 g (1 oz/½ cup) of the mint, the thyme and bay leaves. Scatter over the meat, return to the oven and cook for 15 minutes.

3 Combine the tomato, stock and wine and pour over the meat. Cover tightly with foil or a lid and bake for 1¼ hours. Garnish with the remaining mint and serve with pasta.

Note: This recipe is best made a day or two in advance and refrigerated. This allows the flavours of the dish to develop.

LAMB AND APRICOT STEW

SERVES 4–6

2 kg (4 lb 8 oz) leg lamb, boned
(ask your butcher to do this)

1 onion, thickly sliced

125 ml (4 fl oz/½ cup) white wine

1 tablespoon grated lemon zest

3 tablespoons lemon juice

1 tablespoon ground coriander

4 cardamom pods

1 cinnamon stick

2 tablespoons oil

170 ml (⅔ cup) apricot nectar

90 g (3 oz/½ cup) dried apricots

110 g (4 oz/½ cup) pitted prunes

1 tablespoon cornflour (cornstarch)

80 g (3 oz/½ cup) roasted unsalted
cashew nuts

3 tablespoons finely chopped parsley

1 Trim away the skin and excess fat and cut the meat into 2.5 cm (1 inch) cubes. In a large ceramic or glass bowl, combine the onion, wine, lemon zest, juice, coriander, cardamom pods, cinnamon stick, salt and pepper. Toss the lamb in the marinade, cover and refrigerate for at least 8 hours, or overnight. Stir a few times.

2 Drain meat and onion mixture, reserving the marinade, and dry on paper towels. Discard cardamom and cinnamon. Heat oil in a large heavy-based frying pan and brown the meat and onion in batches, over high heat, for 2–3 minutes.

3 Return all the meat and onion to the pan, then add the marinade and apricot nectar. Bring to the boil, cover with a tight-fitting lid, reduce the heat to low and simmer for 30 minutes; stir once. Stir through the apricots and prunes, cover and simmer for 30 minutes.

4 Mix the cornflour and 1 tablespoon water to a smooth paste. Add to the pan and stir until thickened; simmer for a further 15 minutes, or until the lamb is tender. Scatter with the cashews and parsley and serve with steamed rice.

Variation: Replace the prunes and apricots with dates and sultanas (golden raisins), if preferred.

RICH STEAK AND KIDNEY STEW

SERVES 4-6

1 kg (2 lb 4 oz) chuck steak

2–3 tablespoons oil

1 thick bacon slice, rind removed and thinly sliced

40 g (1½ oz) butter

1 large onion, chopped

300 g (10½ oz) button mushrooms

250 ml (9 fl oz/1 cup) brown muscat or sweet dessert wine (see Note)

2–3 garlic cloves, crushed

¼ teaspoon ground allspice

½ teaspoon paprika

2 teaspoons coriander (cilantro) seeds, lightly crushed

8 lamb kidneys (425 g/15 oz), quartered, cores removed

1 tablespoon wholegrain mustard

250 ml (9 fl oz/1 cup) beef or vegetable stock

2–3 tablespoons soft brown sugar

1–2 teaspoons thyme

1–2 teaspoons rosemary

1 **Trim the steak** of excess fat and sinew; cut into 2–3 cm (¾–1½ inch) cubes. Heat 1 teaspoon of the oil in a large heavy-based pan. Add the bacon and cook for 2–3 minutes until just crisp; remove. Add 2 tablespoons oil and 30 g (1 oz) butter to the pan. Brown steak in batches in the hot oil, then remove from the pan and set aside.

2 **Add the onion** to the pan and cook for 2–3 minutes until soft and golden. Add the mushrooms and cook, stirring, for 3 minutes, until just brown. Stir in half the muscat and simmer for 3–4 minutes. Remove from the pan.

3 **Add remaining oil** and butter to the pan. Stir in the garlic, allspice, paprika and coriander seeds and cook for 1 minute. Add the kidneys and cook, stirring, over medium heat until just beginning to brown. Stir in the remaining muscat and mustard and simmer for 2 minutes. Return the mushroom and onion mixture to the pan, with the steak and bacon, and stir until combined. Stir in the stock. Bring to the boil, reduce the heat, cover and simmer for 1 hour. Stir in the sugar (the amount depends on the sweetness of the muscat), cover and simmer for 40 minutes. Uncover and simmer for 20 minutes. Stir in the thyme and rosemary.

Note: As an alternative, a white wine such as riesling will also work well in this recipe.

TOFU STROGANOFF

SERVES 4

2 tablespoons plain (all-purpose) flour

1 tablespoon paprika

500 g (1 lb 2 oz) firm tofu, cut into
    1.5 cm (½ inch) cubes

1 tablespoon oil

2 teaspoons tomato paste
    (concentrated purée)

3 tablespoons dry sherry

500 ml (17 fl oz/2 cups) vegetable stock

12 baby onions, halved

1 garlic clove, crushed

225 g (8 oz) field mushrooms, cut into
    1 cm (½ in) slices

3 tablespoons sour cream

sour cream, extra, to garnish

2 tablespoons chopped chives

1 **Combine the flour** and paprika in a plastic bag and season well. Add the tofu and shake to coat.

2 **Heat the oil** in a frying pan. Add the tofu and cook over medium heat for 4 minutes, or until golden. Add the tomato paste and cook for another minute. Add 2 tablespoons of the sherry, cook for 30 seconds then transfer the tofu to a bowl. Keep any remaining flour in the pan.

3 **Pour 250 ml** (9 fl oz/1 cup) stock into the pan and bring to the boil. Add onions, garlic and mushrooms. Reduce the heat to medium and simmer, covered, for 10 minutes. Return the tofu to the pan with the remaining sherry and remaining stock. Season to taste. Return to the boil, reduce the heat and simmer for 5 minutes, or until heated through and the sauce has thickened a little.

4 **Remove the pan** from the heat and stir a little of the sauce into the sour cream until smooth and of pouring consistency; return to the pan. Serve garnished with a dollop of the extra sour cream and sprinkle with the chopped chives. This dish is good served with noodles or steamed rice.

FISH WITH HARISSA AND OLIVES

plain (all-purpose) flour for dusting

4 tablespoons olive oil

4 white fish fillets, such as blue eye cod, snapper or perch

1 onion, chopped

2 garlic cloves, crushed

400 g (14 oz) tin chopped tomatoes

2 teaspoons harissa, or to taste (see Note)

2 bay leaves

1 cinnamon stick

175 g (6 oz/1 cup) black olives

1 tablespoon lemon juice

2 tablespoons chopped flat-leaf (Italian) parsley

1 **Season flour** with salt and freshly ground black pepper. Heat half the olive oil in a heavy-based frying pan. Dust the fish fillets with the seasoned flour and add to the pan. Cook the fish over medium heat for 2 minutes on each side, or until golden. Transfer to a plate.

2 **Add remaining olive oil** to the pan and cook the onion and garlic for 3–4 minutes, or until softened. Add the tomato, harissa, bay leaves and cinnamon stick. Cook for 10 minutes, or until the sauce has thickened. Season to taste with salt and freshly ground black pepper.

3 **Return the fish** to the pan, add the olives and cover the fish with the sauce. Remove the bay leaves and cinnamon stick and cook for 2 minutes, or until fish is tender. Add the lemon juice and parsley and serve.

Note: Harissa is a hot chilli paste which is popular in North African cooking.

MUSHROOM RAGU WITH POLENTA

SERVES 4

10 g (¼ oz) dried porcini mushrooms

25 g (1 oz) butter

1 tablespoon olive oil

4 garlic cloves, finely chopped

400 g (14 oz) mixed mushrooms (cap, shiitake, Swiss brown), sliced if large

250 ml (9 fl oz/1 cup) red wine

500 ml (17 fl oz/2 cups) beef stock

3 tablespoons finely chopped parsley

2 teaspoons chopped thyme

100 g (3½ oz) enoki mushrooms

150 g (5½ oz/1 cup) polenta

40 g (1½ oz) butter

4 tablespoons grated parmesan cheese

1 Soak the porcini in 185 ml (6 fl oz/¾ cup) warm water for 15 minutes. Drain and chop, reserving the soaking liquid.

2 Heat the butter and oil in a saucepan, add the garlic and cook over medium heat for 3 minutes. Add the mixed mushrooms and cook for 3 minutes. Stir in the red wine and cook for 5 minutes. Add the porcini, soaking liquid, stock and parsley. Cook over medium heat for 25 minutes, or until the liquid has reduced by half. Stir in the thyme and enoki and keep warm.

3 Bring 1 litre (35 fl oz/4 cups) lightly salted water to the boil in a large saucepan, then reduce the heat to medium. Stir with a wooden spoon to form a whirlpool and add the polenta in a very thin stream. Cook, stirring, for 20 minutes, or until the polenta comes away from the side of the pan. Stir in butter and parmesan, and serve at once with the ragu over the top.

VALENCIAN LAMB AND RICE

SERVES 4-6

100 g (3½ oz/½ cup) chickpeas
1 red onion
1 parsnip
1 celery stalk
1 turnip
200 g (7 oz) diced lamb leg
1 pig's ear, about 150–200 g (5½–7 oz) salted if possible (optional) See Note
100 g (3½ oz) minced (ground) pork
4 tablespoons fine fresh breadcrumbs
50 g (1¾ oz) jamón, finely chopped
1 egg
pinch of ground cinnamon
3 tablespoons chopped flat-leaf (Italian) parsley
1 morcilla or other blood sausage, about 200 g (7 oz)
1 white catalan sausage, butifarra or other mild pork sausage, about 200 g (7 oz)
2 tablespoons olive oil
1 garlic clove, finely chopped
300 g (10½ oz/1⅓ cups) short-grain rice

1 Soak the chickpeas in water for 3–4 hours then drain. Meanwhile chop the onion, parsnip, celery and turnip into 2 cm (¾ in) dice and set aside.

2 Bring 2 litres (70 fl oz/8 cups) water to the boil in a large pot. Add the diced lamb and pig's ear (whole, if using). Bring the water back to boil, then reduce to a steady simmer and cook for 30 minutes. Next add the drained chickpeas, diced onion, parsnip, celery and turnip and season to taste—if the pig's ear was salted you may not need to add any more salt. Continue to simmer for another 20 minutes.

3 Meanwhile combine the pork with the breadcrumbs, jamón, egg, cinnamon and 1 tablespoon of the chopped parsley. Season well. Take heaped teaspoons of mixture and roll into meatballs.

4 Add the whole sausages and the meatballs to the pot. Let mixture return to a simmer and cook for 10 more minutes or until meatballs are firm to the touch and cooked through. Cover and turn off the heat.

5 Preheat oven to 180°C (350°F/Gas 4). Place a heavy-based flameproof casserole dish on the stovetop over medium–high heat. Add the oil and chopped garlic and cook, stirring, for 2 minutes or until the garlic is lightly golden. Add the rice and stir for another minute. Stir in 600 ml (21 fl oz) of the cooking liquid. Bring to the boil, cover and place in oven for 20 minutes or until rice is cooked. Gently reheat stew and serve the rice, garnished with the remaining parsley.

Note: The Spanish meats and sausages used in this dish are available from good delicatessens and continental butchers.

COUNTRY BEEF STEW

SERVES 8

1 small eggplant (aubergine), cubed

2–3 tablespoons olive oil

2 red onions, sliced

2 garlic cloves, crushed

1 kg (2 lb 4 oz) chuck steak, cubed

1 teaspoon ground coriander

½ teaspoon allspice

¾ teaspoon sweet paprika

6 ripe tomatoes, chopped

250 ml (9 fl oz/1 cup) red wine

750 ml (26 fl oz/3 cups) beef stock

2 tablespoons tomato paste
(concentrated purée)

250 g (9 oz) baby potatoes, halved

2 celery stalks, sliced

3 carrots, chopped

2 bay leaves

3 tablespoons chopped parsley

1 Put the eggplant in a colander, sprinkle generously with salt and leave for 20 minutes. Rinse, pat dry with paper towels and set aside.

2 Heat the oil in a large pan. Cook the onion for 5 minutes until soft; add garlic and cook for 1 minute. Remove. Add the eggplant and brown for 5 minutes. Remove. Brown the meat in batches, sprinkle with spices, season and cook for about 2 minutes. Add tomato, onion, wine, stock and paste and bring to the boil. Reduce heat and simmer, covered, for 25 minutes.

3 Add the potato, celery, carrot and bay leaves, bring to the boil, reduce the heat, cover and simmer for 1 hour. Add the eggplant and simmer for 30 minutes, uncovered. Remove the bay leaves and stir in the parsley.

CHILLI CON CARNE

SERVES 6

1 tablespoon olive oil

1 onion, chopped

3 garlic cloves, crushed

2 tablespoons ground cumin

1½ teaspoons chilli powder

600 g (1 lb 5 oz) minced (ground) beef

400 g (14 oz) tin crushed tomatoes

2 tablespoons tomato paste
    (concentrated purée)

2 teaspoons dried oregano

1 teaspoon dried thyme

500 ml (17 fl oz/2 cups) beef stock

1 teaspoon sugar

300 g (10½ oz) tin red kidney beans,
    rinsed and drained

125 g (4½ oz/1 cup) grated cheddar

125 g (4½ oz/½ cup) sour cream

2 tablespoons finely chopped coriander
    (cilantro) leaves

corn chips, to serve

1   **Heat the oil** in a large saucepan over medium heat, add the onion and cook for 5 minutes, or until starting to brown. Add the garlic, cumin, chilli powder and beef, and cook, stirring, for 5 minutes, or until the beef has changed colour. Break up any lumps with the back of a wooden spoon.

2   **Add the tomato,** tomato paste, herbs, beef stock and sugar, and stir to combine. Reduce the heat to low and cook, stirring occasionally, for 1 hour, or until the sauce is rich and thick. Stir in the beans and cook for 2 minutes to heat through.

3   **Divide the chilli** con carne among six serving bowls, sprinkle with the cheese and top with a tablespoon of sour cream. Garnish with the coriander. Serve with corn chips or steamed rice.

BEEF STROGANOFF

SERVES 4

400 g (14 oz) beef fillet, cut into
 1 x 5 cm (½ x 2 in) strips

2 tablespoons plain (all-purpose) flour

50 g (1¾ oz) butter

1 onion, thinly sliced

1 garlic clove, crushed

250 g (9 oz) small Swiss brown
 mushrooms, sliced

3 tablespoons brandy

250 ml (9 fl oz/1 cup) beef stock

1½ tablespoons tomato paste
 (concentrated purée)

185 g (6½ oz/¾ cup) sour cream

1 tablespoon chopped flat-leaf
 (Italian) parsley

1 Dust the beef strips in flour, shaking off any excess.

2 Melt half the butter in a large frying pan and cook the meat in small batches for 1–2 minutes, or until seared all over. Remove. Add the remaining butter to the pan and cook the onion and garlic over medium heat for 2–3 minutes, or until they soften. Add the mushrooms and cook for 2–3 minutes.

3 Pour in the brandy and simmer until nearly all of the liquid has evaporated, then stir in the beef stock and tomato paste. Cook for 5 minutes to reduce the liquid slightly. Return the beef strips to the pan with any juices and stir in the sour cream. Simmer for 1 minute, or until the sauce thickens slightly. Season with salt and freshly ground black pepper.

4 Garnish with the chopped parsley and serve immediately with fettucine or steamed rice.

BOEUF EN DAUBE

SERVES 6

MARINADE

2 cloves

1 onion, cut into quarters

500 ml (17 fl oz/2 cups) red wine

2 strips of orange zest

2 garlic cloves

1 small celery stalk

2 bay leaves

a few parsley stalks

1.5 kg (3 lb 5 oz) beef topside, blade or rump, cut into large pieces

2 tablespoons oil

3 strips pork fat

1 pig's trotter or 225 g (8 oz) piece streaky bacon

750 ml (26 fl oz/3 cups) beef stock

1 To make the marinade, push the cloves into a piece of onion and combine in a large bowl with the rest of the marinade ingredients. Season the beef with salt and pepper, add to the marinade and leave to marinate overnight.

2 Heat the oil in a saucepan. Remove beef from marinade and pat dry, then brown in batches in the oil and remove to a plate. You might need to use a little of the marinade liquid to deglaze the pan between batches to prevent bits sticking to the bottom of the pan and burning.

3 Strain the marinade through a sieve into a bowl and tip the contents of the sieve into the pan to brown. Remove from the pan. Add the marinade liquid to the pan and boil, stirring, for 30 seconds to deglaze the pan.

4 Place the pork fat in a large casserole dish, add the pig's trotter, beef and marinade ingredients. Pour in the marinade liquid and stock. Bring to the boil, then cover, reduce the heat and simmer gently for 2–2½ hours or until the meat is tender. Lift the meat out of the casserole into a serving dish, cover and keep warm. Discard the garlic, onion, pork fat and pig's trotter. Pour the liquid through a fine sieve and skim off as much fat as possible, then return to the casserole dish. Bring to the boil and boil until reduced by half and syrupy. Pour the gravy over the meat to serve.

CHICKEN AND ORANGE CASSEROLE

SERVES 4–6

2 small chickens

1 tablespoon olive oil

2 thick bacon slices, rind removed and thinly sliced

60 g (2 oz) butter

16 small baby onions, peeled (ensure ends are intact)

2–3 garlic cloves, crushed

3 teaspoons grated ginger

2 teaspoons grated orange zest

2 teaspoons ground cumin

2 teaspoons ground coriander

2 tablespoons honey

250 ml (9 fl oz/1 cup) fresh orange juice

250 ml (9 fl oz/1 cup) white wine

125 ml (4 fl oz/½ cup) chicken or vegetable stock

1 bunch baby carrots

1 large parsnip, peeled and cut into thin strips

fresh coriander (cilantro) leaves and orange zest, to serve

1 **Using a sharp knife** or a pair of kitchen scissors, cut each chicken into 8 pieces discarding the backbone. Remove any excess fat and discard (remove the skin as well, if preferred).

2 **Heat about** a teaspoon of the oil in a large, deep heavy-based pan. Add the bacon and cook over medium heat for 2–3 minutes, or until just crisp. Remove from the pan and set aside to drain on paper towels. Add the remaining oil and half the butter to the pan. Cook the onions over medium heat until dark golden brown. Shake the pan occasionally to ensure even cooking and browning. Remove from the pan and set aside.

3 **Add the chicken** pieces to the pan and brown in small batches over medium heat. Remove from the pan and drain.

4 **Add remaining butter** to the pan. Stir in the garlic, ginger, orange zest, cumin, coriander and honey and cook, stirring, for 1 minute. Add the orange juice, wine and stock to the pan.

Bring to the boil and then reduce the heat and simmer for 1 minute. Return the chicken pieces to the pan, cover and leave to simmer over low heat for 40 minutes.

5 **Return the onions** and bacon to the pan and simmer, covered, for a further 15 minutes. Remove the lid and leave to simmer for a further 15 minutes.

6 **Trim carrots**, leaving a little green stalk, and wash well or peel if necessary. Add the carrots and parsnip to the pan. Cover and cook for about 8 minutes or until the carrots and parsnip are just tender. Do not overcook the carrots or they will lose their bright colouring. When you are ready to serve, arrange 2–3 chicken pieces on each plate. Put a couple of carrots and a few parsnip strips on top and spoon over a little juice. Garnish with coriander leaves and orange zest.

MEXICAN BEEF STEW

SERVES 6

500 g (1 lb 2 oz) roma (plum) tomatoes, halved

6 flour tortillas

1–2 red chillies, finely chopped

1 tablespoon olive oil

1 kg (2 lb 4 oz) stewing beef, cubed

2 onions, thinly sliced

375 ml (13 fl oz/1½ cups) beef stock

3 tablespoons tomato paste (concentrated purée)

375 g (13 oz) tin kidney beans, drained

1 teaspoon chilli powder

125 g (4½ oz/½ cup) sour cream

1 **Preheat the oven** to 180°C (350°F/Gas 4). Grill (broil) the tomatoes, skin side up, for 6–8 minutes, or until the skin is black and blistered. Cool, remove the skin and roughly chop the flesh.

2 **Bake two tortillas** for 4 minutes, or until crisp. Break into pieces, put in a food processor with the tomato and chilli and process until almost smooth.

3 **Heat the oil** in a pan. Brown the beef in batches, then remove. Add the onion to the pan; cook for 5 minutes. Return the meat to the pan. Stir in the tomato mixture, stock and tomato paste and bring to the boil. Reduce heat, cover and simmer for 1¼ hours. Add the beans and chilli powder.

4 **Grill (broil)** the remaining tortillas for 3 minutes each side; cool, cut in wedges. Serve with the stew and sour cream.

Note: If this stew becomes thick during cooking, thin with a little extra stock.

CIOPPINO

SERVES 4

1 kg (2 lb 4 oz) firm white-fleshed fish
fillets, skinned and boned

375 g (13 oz) raw king prawns (shrimp)

1 raw lobster tail, in shell

12 fresh mussels

2 dried mushrooms

3 tablespoons olive oil

1 large onion, finely chopped

1 green capsicum (pepper), chopped

2–3 garlic cloves, crushed

425 g (15 oz) tin crushed tomatoes

250 ml (9 fl oz/1 cup) white wine

250 ml (9 fl oz/1 cup) tomato juice

250 ml (9 fl oz/1 cup) fish stock or water

1 bay leaf

2 parsley sprigs

6 basil leaves, chopped

60 g (2 oz/1 cup) chopped parsley

1   Cut fish into bite-size pieces. Remove heads and shells from the prawns, leaving the tails intact, then devein. Remove lobster meat from shell and cut into small pieces. (To make your own stock, simmer the fish, lobster and prawn trimmings in water for 5 minutes, then strain.) Scrub mussels and remove their beards. Discard any open mussels, then soak the rest in cold water for 10 minutes. Soak the mushrooms in water for 20 minutes, squeeze dry and chop finely.

2   Heat the oil in a pan; cook the onion, capsicum and garlic for 5 minutes, or until soft. Add the mushrooms, tomato, wine, tomato juice, stock, bay leaf and herbs. Bring to the boil, then simmer for 30 minutes.

3   Layer the fish and prawns in a large pan, add the sauce, cover and leave on a low heat for 10 minutes, until the prawns are pink and the fish is cooked. Add the lobster and mussels; simmer for 2–3 minutes. Discard any unopened mussels. Sprinkle with parsley.

Notes: Prepare the seafood and sauce several hours prior to cooking. Reheat the sauce, then continue and cook the seafood just prior to serving. You can vary the combination of seafood in this dish to suit your taste or what is available fresh on the day.

MEDITERRANEAN VEGETABLE HOTPOT

SERVES 4

3 tablespoons olive oil

1 onion, chopped

2 garlic cloves, crushed

1 red capsicum (pepper), chopped

1 green capsicum (pepper), chopped

3 slender eggplants (aubergines), sliced

3 zucchini (courgettes), sliced

400 g (14 oz/2 cups) long-grain rice

100 g (3½ oz) button mushrooms, sliced

750 ml (26 fl oz/3 cups) chicken stock

250 ml (9 fl oz/1 cup) white wine

400 g (14 oz) tin crushed tomatoes

2 tablespoons tomato paste
(concentrated purée)

150 g (5½ oz) feta cheese

1 Heat the oil in a pan and cook the onion over medium heat for 10 minutes until very soft but not brown. Add the garlic and cook for a further minute.

2 Add the capsicum, then stir for 3 minutes. Add eggplant and zucchini and stir for 5 minutes, then add the rice, stirring for 2 minutes.

3 Stir in the mushrooms, stock, wine, tomato and paste until combined. Bring to the boil, reduce the heat, cover and simmer for 20 minutes—the rice should absorb most of the liquid. Serve topped with crumbled feta.

Note: If you can, prepare this dish a day ahead and reheat gently. The flavours mature if the dish is made in advance.

CREAMY CHICKEN WITH MUSHROOMS

SERVES 6

2 tablespoons olive oil

200 g (7 oz) button mushrooms, halved

200 g (7 oz) field mushrooms, chopped

1 small red capsicum (pepper), sliced

4 skinless, boneless chicken breasts, cut into bite-sized pieces

2 tablespoons plain (all-purpose) flour

250 ml (9 fl oz/1 cup) chicken stock

125 ml (4 fl oz/½ cup) red wine

3 spring onions (scallions), finely chopped

300 ml (10½ fl oz/1¼ cups) cream

¼ teaspoon ground turmeric

1 tablespoon chopped chives

1 tablespoon finely chopped parsley

1 Heat the oil in a large pan and add the mushrooms and capsicum. Cook over medium heat for 4 minutes or until soft. Remove and set aside.

2 Brown the chicken briefly in batches over medium–high heat. Sprinkle the pan with flour and cook for 2 minutes until golden. Add the stock and wine; bring to the boil. Cover and simmer for 10 minutes, or until the chicken is tender.

3 Add the spring onion and cream, return to the boil and simmer for 10–15 minutes, or until the cream has reduced and thickened. Return the mushrooms and capsicum to the pan; stir in the turmeric and herbs. Season, then simmer for about 5 minutes to heat.

Note: You can use chicken thighs instead of breast for a more economical meal.

CHICKEN WITH PRESERVED LEMON AND OLIVES

SERVES 4

¼ preserved lemon (see Note)

3 tablespoons olive oil

1.6 kg (3 lb 8 oz) chicken

1 onion, chopped

2 garlic cloves, chopped

625 ml (22 fl oz/2½ cups) chicken stock

½ teaspoon ground ginger

1½ teaspoons ground cinnamon

a pinch of saffron threads

100 g (3½ oz/½ cup) unpitted green
olives

2 bay leaves

2 chicken livers

3 tablespoons chopped coriander
(cilantro) leaves

1 **Rinse the preserved lemon** under cold running water, remove and discard the pulp. Drain the rind, pat dry with paper towels and cut into strips. Set aside.

2 **Preheat oven** to 180°C (350°F/Gas 4). Heat 2 tablespoons of the olive oil in a large frying pan, add chicken and brown on all sides. Place in a deep baking dish.

3 **Heat remaining oil,** add the onion and garlic and cook over a medium heat for 3–4 minutes, or until the onion is softened. Add the chicken stock, ginger, cinnamon, saffron, olives, bay leaves and preserved lemon strips and then pour the sauce around the chicken in the dish. Bake for 1½ hours, or until cooked through, adding a little more water or stock if the sauce gets too dry. Baste the chicken during cooking.

4 **Remove the chicken** from the dish, cover with foil and leave to rest. Pour the contents of the baking dish into a frying pan, add chicken livers and mash them into the sauce as they cook. Cook for 5–6 minutes, or until the sauce has reduced and thickened. Add the chopped coriander. Cut the chicken into pieces and serve with the sauce.

Note: Preserved lemons are available in jars from Middle Eastern supermarkets and delicatessens. If unavailable, use fresh lemon rind.

PORK SAUSAGE, SOYA BEAN AND TOMATO CASSEROLE

SERVES 4

325 g (11½ oz/1½ cups) dried soya
    beans, soaked in cold water for at
    least 8 hours, or overnight

8 thin pork sausages (550 g/1 lb 4 oz)

2 tablespoons oil

1 red onion, chopped

4 garlic cloves, chopped

1 large carrot, diced

1 celery stalk, diced

2 x 400 g (14 oz) tins chopped tomatoes

1 tablespoon tomato paste
    (concentrated purée)

250 ml (9 fl oz/1 cup) white wine

2 thyme sprigs

1 teaspoon dried oregano

1 tablespoon oregano, chopped

1 **Drain the soya beans**, place in a large saucepan and cover with fresh water. Bring to the boil, then reduce heat and slowly simmer for 1¼–2 hours—keep the beans covered with water during cooking. Drain. Cook sausages in a lightly oiled frying pan for 10 minutes, or until browned. Drain on paper towels.

2 **Heat oil** in a 3.5 litre (122 fl oz/14 cup) flameproof casserole dish. Add the onion and garlic and cook on the stovetop over a medium heat for 5 minutes. Add carrot and celery and cook, stirring, for 5 minutes. Stir in the tomato, tomato paste, wine, thyme and dried oregano and bring to the boil. Reduce to a simmer, stirring often, for 10 minutes, or until the liquid has reduced and thickened slightly.

3 **Preheat the oven** to 160°C (315°F/Gas 2–3). Add the sausages, beans and 250 ml (9 fl oz/1 cup) water to the casserole dish. Bake, covered, for 2 hours. Stir occasionally, adding more water if necessary to keep the beans just covered.

4 **Return the dish** to the stovetop, skim off any fat, then reduce the liquid until thickened slightly. Remove the thyme sprigs and stir through the oregano.

COUSCOUS WITH LAMB AND SEVEN VEGETABLES

SERVES 4

1 kg (2 lb 4 oz) lamb shoulder, boned
3 tablespoons olive oil
2 onions, quartered
2 garlic cloves, finely chopped
½ teaspoon ground turmeric
½ teaspoon paprika
¼ teaspoon ground saffron threads
4 coriander (cilantro) sprigs
4 flat-leaf (Italian) parsley sprigs
1 cinnamon stick
400 g (14 oz) tin chopped tomatoes
1½ teaspoons freshly ground black pepper
3 carrots, peeled and cut into thick sticks
3 small turnips, peeled and quartered
400 g (14 oz) firm pumpkin (winter squash) or butternut pumpkin (squash)
3 tablespoons raisins
4 zucchini (courgettes), cut into sticks
425 g (15 oz) can chickpeas, rinsed and drained
couscous, to serve
2–3 teaspoons harissa (hot chilli paste), to taste

1 Trim the lamb of excess fat, if necessary. Cut the lamb into 2.5 cm (1 inch) cubes. Heat the oil in a large saucepan or the base of a large couscoussier and add the lamb, onion and garlic. Cook over medium heat, turning the lamb once, just until the lamb loses its red colour. Stir in the turmeric, paprika and saffron and add 750 ml (26 fl oz/3 cups) water. Tie the coriander and parsley in a bunch and add it to the pan, along with the cinnamon stick and tomato. Add the pepper and 1½ teaspoons salt, to taste. Bring to a gentle boil, cover and simmer over low heat for 1 hour. Add the carrot and turnip and cook for a further 20 minutes.

2 Peel the pumpkin and cut it into 2.5 cm (1 inch) chunks. Add the pumpkin to the pan, along with the raisins, zucchini and chickpeas, adding a little water if necessary to almost cover the ingredients.

3 Cook 20 minutes, or until meat and vegetables are tender.

4 Prepare and steam the couscous as directed on the packet, either over the stew or over a saucepan of boiling water, or in the microwave oven.

5 Pile the couscous on a deep, heated platter and make a dent in the centre. Remove the herbs and cinnamon stick from the stew and ladle the meat and vegetables on top of the couscous, letting some tumble down the sides. Moisten with a little broth from the stew. Pour about 250 ml (9 fl oz/1 cup) of the remaining broth into a bowl and stir in the harissa. Add the harissa-flavoured broth to the couscous to keep it moist, according to individual taste.

LAMB CHOP CASSEROLE

SERVES 4

6–8 lamb chump chops

1 teaspoon oil

1 large onion, finely chopped

4 tablespoons redcurrant jelly

1 teaspoon grated lemon zest

1 tablespoon lemon juice

1 tablespoon barbecue sauce

1 tablespoon tomato sauce (ketchup)

125 ml (4 fl oz/ ½ cup) chicken stock

1   Trim any fat from the lamb. Preheat the oven to 170°C (325°F/Gas 3). Heat oil in a large heavy-based frying pan; add the chops and cook over medium–high heat for 3 minutes, turning once, until well browned. Transfer to a casserole dish.

2   Add the onion to the frying pan and cook over medium heat, stirring frequently, for 5 minutes or until the onion is softened. Add the jelly, lemon zest and juice, barbecue and tomato sauces and stock. Stir for 2–3 minutes until heated through. Pour over the chops and stir well, cover and place in the oven. Cook for 1 hour, or until the meat is tender, turning 2–3 times. Lift out the chops onto a side plate and leave them to keep warm.

3   Pour the sauce into a pan and boil rapidly for 5 minutes until the sauce has thickened and reduced. Return the chops to the sauce before serving.

Note: Other cuts of lamb can be used in place of the chump chops, if preferred.

BOSTON BAKED BEANS

SERVES 4–6

350 g (12 oz/1¾ cups) dried cannellini beans

1 whole ham hock

2 onions, chopped

2 tablespoons tomato paste (concentrated purée

1 tablespoon worcestershire sauce

1 tablespoon molasses

1 teaspoon French mustard

3 tablespoons soft brown sugar

125 ml (4 fl oz/½ cup) tomato juice

1 **Cover the beans** with cold water and soak for 6–8 hours, or overnight.

2 **Drain the beans,** rinse them well and place in a large pan. Add the ham hock and cover with cold water. Bring to the boil, then reduce the heat and simmer, covered, for 25 minutes, or until the beans are tender. Preheat the oven to 160°C (315°F/ Gas 2–3).

3 **Remove the ham hock** from the pan and set aside to cool. Drain the beans, reserving 250 ml (9 fl oz/1 cup) of the cooking liquid. Trim the ham of all skin, fat and sinew, then roughly chop the meat and discard the bone.

4 **Transfer the meat** and beans to a 2 litre (70 fl oz/8 cup) casserole dish. Add the reserved liquid and all remaining ingredients. Mix gently, then cover and bake for 1 hour. Serve with hot, buttered toast.

Notes: Any type of dried bean can be used in this recipe. To quick-soak beans, place them in a pan, add hot water to cover and bring slowly to the boil. Remove from the heat and leave to soak for 1 hour before draining and using. Cooked beans can be frozen in small quantities and thawed as needed.

SPICY BEEF, POTATO AND CAPSICUM STEW

SERVES 4–6

300 g (10½ oz) French shallots

2 tablespoons olive oil

1 kg (2 lb 4 oz) gravy beef, cut into 4 cm (1½ inch) cubes

4 garlic cloves, crushed

3 teaspoons paprika

1 teaspoon fennel seeds

½ teaspoon ground cumin

1 tablespoon plain (all-purpose) flour

125 ml (4 fl oz/½ cup) red wine

2 tablespoons brandy

½ teaspoon dried thyme

½ teaspoon dried oregano

1 bay leaf

375 ml (13 fl oz/1½ cups) beef stock

1 tablespoon honey

400 g (14 oz) potatoes, cut into large chunks

2 red capsicums (peppers), chopped

125 g (4½ oz/½ cup) sour cream

chopped chives, for serving

1 **Preheat the oven** to 180°C (350°F/Gas 4). Place shallots in a bowl, cover with boiling water and leave for 30 seconds. Drain and peel.

2 **Heat the oil** in a large, heavy-based pan. Brown the meat in batches over medium–high heat and transfer to a large casserole dish.

3 **Add the shallots** to the pan and cook over medium heat until soft and golden. Add the garlic, paprika, fennel seeds and cumin; cook until fragrant.

4 **Add the flour,** cook for 30 seconds, then remove from the heat. Stir in the red wine and brandy. Return to the heat and add the thyme, oregano, bay leaf and stock. Stir until the mixture bubbles, then add to the meat.

5 **Cover and bake** for 1½ hours, then add the honey, potato and capsicum. Cook, uncovered, for 30 minutes, or until the potato is tender. Season to taste. Serve with a dollop of sour cream and a sprinkling of chives.

SERVES 4–6

2 tablespoons olive oil

1 kg (2 lb 4 oz) stewing beef, cut into large cubes

2 red onions, sliced

4 garlic cloves, crushed

1 teaspoon cumin seeds

2 teaspoons ground cumin

1 teaspoon ground coriander

2 teaspoons sweet paprika

1 tablespoon plain (all-purpose) flour

500 ml (17 fl oz/2 cups) beef stock

1 teaspoon grated lemon zest

1 tablespoon soft brown sugar

1 tablespoon tomato paste (concentrated purée)

3 tablespoons lemon juice

4 fresh globe artichokes

3 tablespoons small black olives

1 **Preheat the oven** to 180°C (350°F/Gas 4). Heat half the oil in a large heavy-based pan. Brown the meat in batches over medium–high heat and transfer to a large casserole dish.

2 **Add the remaining** oil to the pan and cook the onion over medium heat for 5 minutes, or until soft. Add the garlic, cumin seeds, cumin, coriander and paprika and cook for 1 minute.

3 **Add the flour,** cook for 30 seconds and remove from the heat. Add the stock, return to the heat and stir until the mixture bubbles. Add to the meat with the zest, sugar and tomato paste. Cover tightly and bake for 1½ hours.

4 **Add the lemon** juice to a bowl of water. Cut the top third from each artichoke, trim the stem to 5 cm (2 inch) and cut away the dark outer leaves. Cut the artichokes lengthways in half. Remove the prickly lavender-topped leaves in the centre and scoop out the hairy choke. Drop into the lemon-water until ready to use.

5 **Drain the artichokes** and add to the casserole, covering them in the liquid. Cover and cook for 30 minutes, or until tender. For a thicker gravy, cook uncovered for 15 minutes more. Season and stir in the olives to serve.

PEPPERCORN STEW

SERVES 4

1 kg (2 lb 4 oz) chuck steak, cut into
  3 cm (1¼ inch) cubes

2 teaspoons cracked black peppercorns

40 g (1½ oz) butter

2 tablespoons oil

1 large onion, thinly sliced

2 garlic cloves, sliced

1½ tablespoons plain (all-purpose) flour

2 tablespoons brandy

750 ml (26 fl oz/3 cups) beef stock

1 tablespoon worcestershire sauce

2 teaspoons dijon mustard

500 g (1 lb 2 oz) baby potatoes

3 tablespoons cream

2 tablespoons chopped parsley

1   Toss the steak in the peppercorns. Heat half the butter and half the oil in a large heavy-based pan. Brown half the steak over high heat; remove and set aside. Heat the remaining butter and oil and brown the remaining steak. Remove and set aside.

2   Add the onion and garlic to the pan and cook, stirring, until the onion is golden. Add the flour and stir until browned. Remove from the heat.

3   Combine the brandy, beef stock, worcestershire sauce and mustard, and gradually stir into the onion mixture. Return to the heat, add the steak and any juices, then simmer, covered, for 1¼ hours.

4   Add the potatoes and simmer, uncovered, for a further 30 minutes, or until the meat and potatoes are tender. Stir in the cream and parsley. Season to taste with salt and freshly ground black pepper.

VEAL WITH SWEET VEGETABLES

SERVES 4

olive oil, for cooking

8 veal shank pieces, each 2 cm (¾ inch) thick

2 garlic cloves, finely chopped

2 onions, chopped

2 carrots, chopped

1 celery stalk, chopped

2 bay leaves, torn

750 ml (26 fl oz/3 cups)) beef stock

200 g (7 oz) white sweet potato

200 g (7 oz) parsnips

150 g (5½ oz) baby turnips

50 g (1¾ oz) butter

150 g (5½ oz) baby potatoes

2 teaspoons soft brown sugar

2 tablespoons balsamic vinegar

1 **Preheat the oven** to 160°C (315°F/Gas 2–3). Heat 3 tablespoons of oil in a roasting tin over medium heat and brown the veal all over. Remove and set aside. Add the garlic, onion, carrot and celery and brown lightly for 10 minutes. Add the veal, bay leaves and stock and stir well. Bring to the boil, cover tightly with foil, then bake for 1½ hours.

2 **Towards the end** of baking, cut the sweet potato and parsnips into large chunks; trim the turnips and cut in half. Heat the butter and a little oil in a deep frying pan until foamy. Toss all the root vegetables over medium heat for 5–6 minutes, or until the edges are golden. Sprinkle with sugar and vinegar and toss well. Cook gently for 10 minutes, or until the vegetables soften and the juices caramelise.

3 **Turn veal** in the stock, add the vegetables and toss well. If the meat is drying out, stir in 250 ml (9 fl oz/1 cup) water. Season well, then cover and cook for 20 minutes. Serve with steamed rice or creamy polenta.

BEEF SAUSAGE AND MUSHROOM STEW

SERVES 4–6

15 g (½ oz) packet dried porcini mushrooms

12 thick beef sausages

300 g (10½ oz) piece speck or bacon (see Note)

2 teaspoons oil

2 onions, cut into eighths

8 garlic cloves

1 thyme sprig

3 bay leaves

375 ml (13 fl oz/1½ cups) red wine

250 ml (9 fl oz/1 cup) beef stock

1 teaspoon dijon mustard

1 bunch baby carrots

100 g (3½ oz) Swiss brown mushrooms, halved

100 g (3½ oz) button mushrooms, halved

1 tablespoon cornflour (cornstarch)

chopped parsley, for serving

1 Soak the porcini mushrooms for 30 minutes in enough boiling water to cover.

2 Brown the sausages well all over in a lightly oiled pan over medium heat. Drain on paper towels and place in a large, flameproof casserole dish.

3 Remove the rind from the speck or bacon; cut the meat into small strips. Heat oil in a pan and add the speck, onions and garlic. Cook, stirring, until the onions are golden, then place in the casserole dish with the thyme, bay leaves, wine, stock and mustard. Cover, bring to the boil, then reduce the heat and simmer for 20 minutes.

4 Reserving 3 tablespoons of liquid, drain the mushrooms. Add the carrots and all mushrooms to the stew. Cover and simmer for 20 minutes. Mix the cornflour into the reserved liquid; stir into the stew until it boils and thickens. Sprinkle with parsley to serve.

Note: Speck is a type of smoked bacon sold in delicatessens.

ROSEMARY-INFUSED LAMB AND LENTIL CASSEROLE

SERVES 6

25 g (1 oz) butter

2 tablespoons olive oil

1 onion, finely sliced

2 garlic cloves, crushed

1 small carrot, finely chopped

2 teaspoons cumin seeds

¼ teaspoon chilli flakes

2 teaspoons finely chopped ginger

1 kg (2 lb 4 oz) boned leg of lamb,
cut into 4 cm (1½ inch) cubes

2 teaspoons rosemary

750 ml (26 fl oz/3 cups) lamb or chicken
stock

185 g (6½ oz/1 cup) green or brown
lentils

3 teaspoons soft brown sugar

2 teaspoons balsamic vinegar

1 **Preheat the oven** to 180°C (350°F/Gas 4). Heat the butter and half the oil in a large, heavy-based pan. Add onion, garlic and carrot and cook over medium heat for about 5 minutes, or until soft and golden. Add the cumin seeds, chilli flakes and ginger. Cook for 1 minute. Transfer to a large casserole dish.

2 **Heat the remaining** oil in the pan and brown the lamb in batches over high heat. Transfer to the casserole dish.

3 **Add rosemary** to pan. Stir in 625 ml (21½ fl oz/2½ cups) of the stock, scraping up all the brown bits from the base and side of the pan. Heat until the stock is bubbling, then pour into the casserole dish. Cover and bake for 1 hour.

4 **Add the lentils,** sugar and vinegar and cook for a further 1 hour, or until the lentils are cooked. If the mixture is too thick, stir in the remaining stock. Season with salt and freshly ground black pepper.

CASSEROLE OF AUTUMN VEGETABLES

SERVES 4–6

185 g (6½ oz) frozen broad (fava) beans, thawed (see Notes)

150 g (5 oz) baby onions

50 g (1¾ oz) butter

2 teaspoons olive oil

400 g (14 oz) small parsnips

150 g (5½ oz) Jerusalem artichokes

2 tablespoons plain (all-purpose) flour

600 ml (20 fl oz/2⅓ cups chicken stock

300 ml (10½ fl oz) cream

2 teaspoons grated lemon zest

1 teaspoon grated orange zest

400 g (14 oz) baby carrots, trimmed

500 g (1 lb 2 oz) baby turnips, trimmed

1 Peel and discard the tough outer skin of the broad beans. Carefully peel the onions, leaving the flat root end attached, then cut a cross through the root end of each onion.

2 Heat the butter and oil in a large, heavy-based pan until foamy. Add onions and cook for 7 minutes over low–medium heat, turning often to colour evenly.

3 While the onions are browning, peel the parsnips and artichokes and cut into bite-sized pieces. Add to the pan and toss well. Scatter with the flour, toss to coat and cook for 2 minutes.

4 Stir in the stock, cream and zests. Bring to the boil, stirring, then reduce heat and simmer for 7 minutes, or until vegetables are half-cooked.

5 Add the carrots and turnips; toss well. Cover and cook for 5 minutes, or until the vegetables are just tender. Season well with salt and freshly ground pepper, stir in the broad beans to heat through, and serve.

Notes: Baby vegetables have a sweet, delicate flavour. If they are unavailable, choose the smallest vegetables you can find and cook them for a few minutes longer than stated in the recipe. Fresh broad beans can be used in place of frozen. Add them with the carrots and turnips.

LENTIL BHUJIA STEW

SERVES 4–6

2 cups (370 g/12 oz) green or brown lentils

1 large onion, grated

1 large potato, grated

1 teaspoon ground cumin

1 teaspoon ground coriander

1 teaspoon ground turmeric

100 g (3½ oz/⅔ cup) plain flour

oil, for shallow-frying

2 garlic cloves, crushed

1 tablespoon grated ginger

250 ml (9 fl oz/1 cup) tomato passata (puréed tomatoes)

500 ml (17 fl oz/2 cups) vegetable stock

250 ml (9 fl oz/1 cup) cream

200 g (7 oz) green beans, topped, tailed and cut in half

2 carrots, sliced

2 hard-boiled eggs, chopped

1 Soak the lentils overnight in cold water. Drain well. Squeeze the excess moisture from the lentils, onion and potato using a tea towel (dish towel). Place in a bowl with the ground spices and flour; combine well and leave for 10 minutes. With floured hands, shape the mixture into walnut-sized balls and place on a foil-lined tray. Cover and refrigerate for 30 minutes.

2 Heat 2 cm (¾ inch) of oil in a heavy-based pan. Cook the balls in batches over high heat until golden brown. Drain on paper towels.

3 Heat 2 tablespoons of oil in a pan; gently fry the garlic and ginger for 2 minutes. Stir in the passata, stock and cream. Bring to the boil, reduce heat and simmer for 10 minutes. Add the beans, lentil balls and carrots. Cook, covered, for 30 minutes, stirring twice. Add egg and cook for 10 minutes.

Variation: Split peas can be used in this recipe in place of the lentils. Soak them in cold water overnight, then drain well before using.

CHICKEN CACCIATORE

SERVES 4

1.25 kg (2 lb 12 oz) chicken pieces

2 tablespoons plain (all-purpose) flour

1 tablespoon olive oil

1 large onion, finely chopped

2 garlic cloves, chopped

2 x 425 g (15 oz) tins tomatoes, roughly chopped

500 ml (17 fl oz/2 cups) chicken stock

125 ml (4 fl oz/½ cup) white wine

2 tablespoons tomato paste (concentrated purée)

1 teaspoon caster (superfine) sugar

2 tablespoons chopped basil

2 tablespoons chopped parsley

90 g (3¼ oz/½ cup) black olives

1 **Toss the chicken** in the flour to coat. Heat the oil in a large, heavy-based pan and brown the chicken in batches over medium heat. Remove the chicken from the pan and drain on paper towels.

2 **Cook the onion** and garlic in the pan for 10 minutes over low heat, stirring. Add the tomato, stock and wine. Bring to the boil, reduce the heat and simmer for 15 minutes. Add the tomato paste, sugar and chicken; mix well.

3 **Cover and simmer** for 30 minutes, then add the herbs and olives and season to taste. Simmer for another 15 minutes, stirring occasionally.

CHICKEN FRICASSÉE

SERVES 4

25 g (1 oz) butter

1 tablespoon olive oil

200 g (7 oz) button mushrooms, sliced

1.5 kg (3 lb 5 oz) chicken pieces

1 onion, chopped

2 celery stalks, sliced

250 ml (9 fl oz/1 cup) dry white wine

250 ml (9 fl oz/1 cup) chicken stock

1 bay leaf

250 ml (9 fl oz/1 cup) cream

1 kg (2 lb 4 oz) King Edward or russet
    potatoes, peeled and chopped

170 ml (5½ fl oz/⅔ cup) milk, heated

70 g butter, extra

2 tablespoons chopped fresh parsley

1 Heat half the butter and oil in a large saucepan. Add the mushrooms and cook over medium heat for 5 minutes, or until soft and golden. Remove from the pan with a slotted spoon. Heat the remaining oil and butter, add the chicken pieces in batches and cook for 4 minutes, or until browned. Remove from the pan.

2 Add onion and celery to the pan, and cook for 8 minutes, or until soft. Pour in the white wine and stir well. Add stock, chicken, mushrooms, bay leaf and cream. Bring to the boil, then reduce heat and simmer, covered, for about 40 minutes, or until the chicken is cooked through and tender.

3 Bring a large saucepan of water to the boil, add the potato and cook for 10 minutes, or until tender. Drain, add the milk and extra butter, and mash with a potato masher until smooth. Season with salt and freshly ground black pepper.

4 Add the chopped parsley to the chicken and season. Serve with mashed potato.

BEEF WITH GUINNESS

SERVES 4–6

1 kg (2 lb 4 oz) round steak

30 g (1 oz) butter

1 tablespoon olive oil

2 large onions, chopped

2 tablespoons plain (all-purpose) flour

250 ml (9 fl oz/1 cup) Guinness, or other dark beer (see Note)

250 ml (9 fl oz/1 cup) beef stock

3 large carrots, peeled and cut into 3 cm (1¼ inch) pieces

2 large parsnips, peeled and cut into 3 cm (1¼ inch) pieces

2 bay leaves

1 handful chopped parsley

1 **Preheat the oven to** 160°C (315°F/Gas 2–3). Trim the meat of fat and sinew. Cut into 2.5 cm (1 inch) cubes.

2 **Heat the butter** and oil in a large frying pan; add meat in small batches and cook for 4–5 minutes or until browned on all sides. Remove meat from pan and place in a casserole dish.

3 **Add the onion** to the pan and cook gently for 3–4 minutes or until brown. Add flour and stir over low heat for 2 minutes or until the flour is lightly golden.

4 **Add the combined Guinness** and stock gradually to the pan, stirring until the mixture is smooth. Stir constantly over a medium heat for 2 minutes or until the mixture boils and thickens; boil for another minute. Place carrots, parsnips and bay leaves in the casserole dish. Pour the sauce over. Cover and cook for 1½ hours or until the meat and vegetables are tender. Sprinkle the parsley on top just before serving.

Variations: Replace round steak with chuck steak. A boned leg of lamb, cut into 3 cm (1¼ inch) cubes, may be substituted for beef steak. Half a cup of prunes, halved and pitted, can be added during the final 30 minutes of cooking. The prunes will add sweetness to the recipe.

Note: Guinness is a traditional Irish draught stout. It has a strong, bitter taste and is dark in colour. When added to beef dishes, it gives the meat a very distinctive taste. You may find the taste of Guinness too strong. If this is the case, a lighter ale may be used as a substitute in this recipe.

OSSO BUCO WITH GREMOLATA

SERVES 4–6

12 meaty pieces veal shank, osso buco style

4 tablespoons plain (all-purpose) flour, seasoned

20 g (½ oz) butter

4 tablespoons olive oil

1 onion, diced

1 carrot, diced

1 celery stalk, diced

1 bay leaf

1 garlic clove, crushed

500 ml (17 fl oz/2 cups) veal or chicken stock

250 ml (9 fl oz/1 cup) white wine

4 tablespoons lemon juice

GREMOLATA

12 g (¼ oz/⅔ cup) flat-leaf (Italian) parsley, finely chopped

2 garlic cloves, finely chopped

1 tablespoon grated lemon zest

1 Lightly dust the veal shanks in the seasoned flour. Heat the butter and 3 tablespoons oil in a large deep-sided frying pan over high heat until sizzling. Add veal and cook in batches for 5 minutes, or until brown all over. Remove from the pan.

2 Heat remaining oil in a large saucepan and add the onion, carrot, celery and bay leaf, and cook for 10 minutes, or until softened and starting to brown. Stir in the garlic, stock, wine and lemon juice, scraping the bottom of the pan to remove any sediment. Add the veal, bring to the boil, then reduce the heat to low, cover and simmer for 1½–2 hours, or until the veal is very tender and falling off the bone and the sauce has reduced. Season to taste.

3 To make the gremolata, combine the parsley, garlic and zest. Sprinkle over the osso bucco just before serving. Serve with soft polenta.

CHICKEN AND VEGETABLE HOT POT

SERVES 4

8 boneless, skinless chicken thighs
(about 1.3 kg/3 lb)

75 g (2½ oz/½ cup) unsifted all-purpose
flour

2 tablespoons oil

1 medium onion, sliced

1 garlic clove, finely chopped

4 bacon slices, chopped

2 potatoes, peeled and cut into 2 cm
(¾ in) cubes

1 large carrot, sliced

1 celery stalk, sliced

2 zucchini (courgettes), sliced

250 g (9 oz) cauliflower florets

400 g (14 oz) tin crushed tomatoes

3 tablespoons tomato paste
(concentrated purée)

185 ml (6 fl oz/¾ cup) dry red wine

185 ml (6 fl oz/¾ cup) chicken stock

1 Trim the chicken thighs of excess fat and sinew. Combine the flour and some ground black pepper. Toss chicken lightly in the seasoned flour and shake off excess.

2 Heat the oil in a large frying pan. Cook the chicken over medium heat, turning occasionally, until browned, cooked through and no longer pink near the bone (about 20 minutes). Drain on paper towels; keep warm.

3 Add sliced onion, garlic and bacon to the pan. Cook and stir over medium–high heat, until the onion is tender. Drain fat. Add the potato, carrot and celery; cook, stirring, for about 2 minutes. Add the zucchini, cauliflower, undrained crushed tomatoes, tomato paste, wine and stock. Season to taste.

4 Bring to the boil; reduce heat. Simmer, covered, for about 10 minutes, stirring occasionally, or until vegetables are tender. Do not overcook. Add the chicken to the sauce mixture and cook, uncovered, for 5 minutes or until heated through.

RUSTIC HOT POT

SERVES 4

2 tablespoons olive oil

8 lamb shanks

2 onions, sliced

4 garlic cloves, finely chopped

3 bay leaves, torn in half

1–2 teaspoons hot paprika

2 teaspoons sweet paprika

1 tablespoon plain (all-purpose) flour

3 tablespoons tomato paste (concentrated purée)

1.5 litres (44 fl oz/6 cups) vegetable stock

4 potatoes, chopped

4 carrots, sliced

3 celery stalks, thickly sliced

3 tomatoes, seeded and chopped

1 **To make the** lamb stock, heat 1 tablespoon of the oil in a large, heavy-based pan over medium heat. Brown the shanks well in two batches and drain on paper towels

2 **Add the remaining oil** to the pan. Cook onion, garlic and bay leaves over a low heat for 10 minutes, stirring regularly. Add the paprikas and flour and cook, stirring continuously, for 2 minutes. Gradually add combined tomato paste and stock. Bring to the boil, stirring continuously, and return shanks to the pan. Simmer over low heat, covered, for 1½ hours, stirring the mixture occasionally.

3 **Remove the bay** leaves and discard. Remove the shanks, allow to cool slightly and then cut the meat from the bone. Discard the bones. Cut the meat into pieces and refrigerate. Refrigerate the stock for about 1 hour, or until fat forms on the surface and can be spooned off.

4 **Return the meat** to the hot pot along with the potato, carrot and celery and bring to the boil. Reduce the heat and simmer for 15 minutes. Season and add the chopped tomato just before serving.

SLOW COOKERS

CREAMY TOMATO AND CHICKEN STEW

SERVES 4

1.5 kg (3 lb 5 oz) chicken pieces, trimmed of excess fat

4 bacon slices, fat removed, roughly chopped

2 onions, chopped

1 garlic clove, crushed

400 g (14 oz) tin chopped tomatoes

300 g (10½ oz) small button mushrooms, halved

250 ml (9 fl oz/1 cup) cream

2 tablespoons chopped flat-leaf (Italian) parsley

1 tablespoon fresh lemon thyme

1 **Put the chicken,** bacon, onion, garlic and tomatoes in the slow cooker. Cook on high for 3 hours, or until the chicken is nearly tender.

2 **Add the mushrooms** and cream and cook for 30 minutes, then remove the lid and cook for a further 30 minutes to thicken the sauce. Stir through the lemon thyme and parsley. Serve with mashed potatoes and green beans.

LAMB CHOPS IN RATATOUILLE

SERVES 4–6

1 kg (2 lb 4 oz) lamb forequarter chops

1 eggplant (aubergine), cut into
   2 cm (¾ inch) cubes

1 red capsicum (pepper), cut into
   2 cm (¾ inch) cubes

1 green capsicum (pepper), cut into
   2 cm (¾ inch) cubes

1 red onion, cut into 1 cm (½ inch)
   cubes

2 tablespoons capers

4 anchovies, chopped

80 g (2¾ oz/½ cup) pitted kalamata
   olives, chopped

3 tablespoons tomato paste
   (concentrated purée)

2 garlic cloves, chopped

400 g (14 oz) tin chopped tomatoes

150 g (5½ oz/¾ cup) Israeli couscous
   (see Note)

1 small handful flat-leaf (Italian) parsley,
   chopped

1 **Trim the lamb** chops of excess fat and cut into pieces. Put the eggplant, red and green capsicum, onion, capers, anchovies, olives, tomato paste, garlic and tomato in the slow cooker. Put the lamb chops on top and cook on low for 6–6½ hours, or until the lamb is tender, stirring occasionally.

2 **Stir in the couscous** and continue to cook for another 1 hour, or until the couscous is tender and cooked through.

3 **Season with salt** and freshly ground black pepper, and sprinkle with parsley just before serving.

Note: Israeli couscous is larger in size than the more familiar Moroccan couscous, and has a chewier texture. It is sold in most gourmet food stores and health food stores.

LAMB SHANKS IN RED WINE

SERVES 4

1 onion, finely diced

1 leek, white part only, finely diced

1 carrot, finely diced

2 celery stalks, finely diced

1.4 kg (3 lb 2 oz) lamb shanks (4 shanks, about 350 g/12 oz each)

3 garlic cloves, sliced

4 large rosemary sprigs

4 prosciutto slices

3 tablespoons tomato paste (concentrated purée)

500 ml (17 fl oz/2 cups) beef stock

250 ml (9 fl oz/1 cup) red wine

90 g (3¼ oz/½ cup) black olives

1 small handful flat-leaf (Italian) parsley, finely chopped

1   **Place diced vegetables** in the base of the slow cooker.

2   **Make three or four** small incisions in the meaty part of the lamb shanks. Insert garlic slices in the incisions. Place a rosemary sprig on each lamb shank and wrap it with a slice of prosciutto. Secure the prosciutto with a toothpick.

3   **Add the lamb** shanks to the diced vegetables in the slow cooker. Top with the tomato paste, stock and wine and season with salt and freshly ground black pepper. Cook on high for 4½ hours.

4   **Add olives** and cook, uncovered, for a further 5 minutes, or until the olives are warmed through. Stir through the parsley and serve.

LAMB WITH GREEN OLIVES AND PRESERVED LEMON

SERVES 4

½ preserved lemon or peel from
  ½ lemon

1 kg (2 lb 4 oz) lamb forequarter chops

1 onion, sliced

2 garlic cloves, crushed

2 cm (¾ inch) piece ginger, finely diced

1 teaspoon ground cumin

½ teaspoon ground turmeric

130 g (4½ oz/¾ cup) green olives

625 ml (21 fl oz/2½ cups) chicken stock

400 g (14 oz) all-purpose potatoes, cut
  into 2 cm (¾ inch) dice

2 tablespoons chopped flat-leaf (Italian)
  parsley

2 tablespoons chopped coriander
  (cilantro) leaves

1 Rinse the preserved lemon well, remove and discard the pulp and membrane and finely dice the rind.

2 Trim the lamb of any excess fat and cut each chop in half.

3 Put the lemon, lamb chops, onion, garlic, ginger, cumin, turmeric, olives and stock in the slow cooker. Cook on high for 2 hours. Add the potato and half the combined parsley and coriander leaves and cook for a further 1 hour, or until lamb is tender and the potato is cooked.

4 Stir in remaining parsley and coriander and season to taste with salt and freshly ground black pepper. Serve with rice.

LANCASHIRE HOTPOT

SERVES 4

4 all-purpose potatoes, sliced

6 baby onions, peeled and left whole

1 tablespoon thyme, chopped

1 kg (2 lb 4 oz) lamb shoulder chops

2 tablespoons worcestershire sauce

125 ml (4 fl oz/½ cup) beef stock

1 handful flat-leaf (Italian) parsley, chopped

1 **In a large bowl**, toss together the potato, onions and thyme. Layer potato and onions in the base of the slow cooker and top with the lamb chops. Pour over the worcestershire sauce and stock. Cook on high for 4 hours, or until the lamb is tender and cooked through.

2 **Season with salt** and freshly ground black pepper, and stir through the parsley just before serving.

POLENTA AND VEGETABLE HOTPOT

SERVES 4–6

2 tablespoons olive oil

300 g (10½ oz/2 cups) polenta

¼ teaspoon paprika

pinch of cayenne pepper

1 teaspoon salt

1.5 litres (52 fl oz/6 cups) vegetable stock or water

3 spring onions (scallions), chopped

1 large tomato, chopped

1 zucchini (courgette), chopped

1 red or green capsicum (pepper), seeded and chopped

300 g (10½ oz) pumpkin (winter squash), peeled and cut into 1.5 cm (¼ inch) dice

100 g (3½ oz) button mushrooms, chopped

300 g (10½ oz) tin corn kernels, drained

100 g (3½ oz/1 cup) grated parmesan cheese

1 handful flat-leaf (Italian) parsley, chopped

125 ml (4 fl oz/½ cup) cream (optional)

1   Pour 1 tablespoon of the olive oil into the slow cooker and spread it over the base and side. Pour in polenta, then add the paprika, cayenne pepper, salt and freshly ground black pepper. Stir in the stock and remaining oil. Stir to combine.

2   Add the spring onion, tomato, zucchini, capsicum, pumpkin, mushrooms and corn and mix well. Cook on high for 2–3 hours, or until the polenta is soft and the vegetables are cooked. Stir several times with a fork to keep the polenta from setting on the base. Start checking after 2 hours to see if the vegetables are tender.

3   Before serving, stir through the parmesan and parsley. For a richer taste, stir through the cream, if using. Taste and season with salt and freshly ground black pepper, if necessary. Serve with a green salad.

NAVARIN OF LAMB

SERVES 4

1 kg (2 lb 4 oz) boneless lean lamb
    shoulder

200 g (7 oz) baby turnips

8 bulb spring onions (scallions), trimmed

175 g (6 oz) small potatoes, peeled
    (halved if large)

1 onion, chopped

1 garlic clove, crushed

125 ml (4 fl oz/½ cup) chicken stock

125 ml (4 fl oz/½ cup) red wine

2 tablespoons tomato paste
    (concentrated purée)

1 large rosemary sprig

2 thyme sprigs

1 bay leaf

18 baby carrots

155 g (5½ oz/1 cup) fresh or frozen peas

1 tablespoon redcurrant jelly

1 handful flat-leaf (Italian) parsley,
    chopped

1 **Trim the lamb** of any excess fat and cut into 2.5 cm
(1 inch) cubes. Put lamb, turnips, spring onions, potatoes,
onion, garlic, stock, wine, tomato paste, rosemary, thyme and
bay leaf in the slow cooker. Stir to combine. Cook on high for
3 hours, or until the lamb is almost tender.

2 **Trim the carrots,** leaving a little bit of green stalk. Add the
carrots to the slow cooker and cook for a further 40 minutes,
or until the carrots are tender.

3 **Stir through** the peas, redcurrant jelly and parsley and
cook for a further 5 minutes, or until the peas are tender.
Season with salt and freshly ground black pepper and serve.

AFRICAN-STYLE LAMB AND PEANUT STEW

SERVES 4—6

1 kg (2 lb 4 oz) lamb (such as boneless lamb leg steaks)

3 teaspoons curry powder

1 teaspoon dried oregano

pinch of cayenne pepper

1 large onion, chopped

1 large carrot, chopped

1 red capsicum (pepper), seeded and chopped

4 garlic cloves, chopped

1 red or green chilli, seeded and finely chopped

500 g (1 lb 2 oz) orange sweet potato, cut into 2.5 cm (1 inch) cubes

400 g (14 oz) tin chopped tomatoes

125 ml (4 fl oz/½ cup) tomato sauce (ketchup)

2 bay leaves

4 tablespoons crunchy or smooth peanut butter

1 tablespoon lemon juice

165 ml (5½ fl oz) tinned coconut milk

155 g (5½ oz/1 cup) fresh or frozen peas

1   Trim the lamb of any fat and cut into 2.5 cm (1 inch) cubes. Put lamb in a large bowl and sprinkle over the curry powder, oregano and cayenne pepper. Season with salt and freshly ground black pepper. Toss well to coat the lamb.

2   Add the onion, carrot, capsicum, garlic, chilli, sweet potato, tomato, tomato sauce and bay leaves to the lamb. Toss to thoroughly combine all the ingredients. Transfer the lamb and vegetables to the slow cooker. Cook on high for 4–6 hours, or until the lamb and vegetables are tender and cooked through.

3   Meanwhile, combine peanut butter, lemon juice and coconut milk in a small bowl. During the last 30 minutes of cooking, add peanut butter mixture to the slow cooker and stir to combine the ingredients. Add the peas and cook for 5 minutes, or until tender.

PERSIAN LAMB WITH CHICKPEAS

SERVES 4–6

750 g (1 lb 10 oz) boneless lamb leg or shoulder

1 teaspoon ground cinnamon

1 teaspoon allspice

1 teaspoon freshly grated nutmeg

1 large onion, chopped

2 garlic cloves, chopped

200 g (7 oz) eggplant (aubergine), cut into 2 cm (¾ inch) dice

1 carrot, chopped

1 zucchini (courgette), chopped

400 g (14 oz) tin chopped tomatoes

3 tablespoons lemon juice

1 tablespoon tomato paste (concentrated purée)

400 g (14 oz) tin chickpeas, drained and rinsed

90 g (3¼ oz/¾ cup) raisins

60 g (2¼ oz/½ cup) slivered almonds, toasted

1 small handful mint, to garnish

1 **Trim lamb** of excess fat and cut into 2.5 cm (1 inch) cubes. Put the lamb in the slow cooker, sprinkle over the cinnamon, allspice and nutmeg and season with salt and freshly ground black pepper. Stir to combine. Stir in onion, garlic, eggplant, carrot and zucchini.

2 **Pour in** the tomato and lemon juice and add the tomato paste. Add the chickpeas and raisins and stir well. Cook for 4–6 hours, or until the lamb is very tender.

3 **To serve,** spoon into serving bowls and scatter over the almonds and mint leaves. Serve with basmati rice and plain yoghurt if desired.

PORTUGUESE BEEF

SERVES 6

1.25 kg (2 lb 12 oz) chuck steak

2 garlic cloves, thinly sliced

175 g (6 oz) smoked bacon slices, chopped

250 ml (9 fl oz/1 cup) red wine

250 ml (9 fl oz/1 cup) beef stock

1 tablespoon sweet paprika

¾ teaspoon smoked paprika

2 bay leaves

2 teaspoons dried oregano

20 g (¾ oz) butter, at room temperature

2 tablespoons plain (all-purpose) flour

175 g (6 oz/1 cup) green olives

3 tablespoons slivered almonds

1   Trim the beef and cut into 4 cm (1½ inch) cubes. Put the beef, garlic, bacon, wine, stock, sweet paprika, smoked paprika, bay leaves and oregano in the slow cooker. Cook on low for 5 hours, or until the beef is tender.

2   Combine butter and flour. Add gradually to the beef in the slow cooker, stirring. Cook, uncovered, for 10 minutes, or until the mixture has thickened.

3   Stir in the olives and almonds and season with salt and freshly ground black pepper. Serve with mashed potato or steamed rice.

BEEF STEW

SERVES 6–8

1 kg (2 lb 4 oz) chuck, blade or skirt steak

1 small eggplant (aubergine), cut into 1.5 cm (½ inch) cubes

250 g (9 oz) baby potatoes, halved

2 celery stalks, sliced

3 carrots, chopped

2 red onions, sliced

6 ripe tomatoes, chopped

2 garlic cloves, crushed

1 teaspoon ground coriander

½ teaspoon allspice

¾ teaspoon sweet paprika

250 ml (9 fl oz/1 cup) red wine

500 ml (17 fl oz/2 cups) beef stock

2 tablespoons tomato paste (concentrated purée)

2 bay leaves

3 tablespoons flat-leaf (Italian) parsley, chopped

1 **Trim beef** and cut it into 4 cm (1½ inch) cubes. Put the beef in the slow cooker along with the eggplant, potato, celery, carrot, onion, tomato, garlic, coriander, allspice, paprika, wine, stock, tomato paste and bay leaves. Cook on low for 5½ hours, or until the beef is tender and cooked through.

2 **Season to taste** with salt and freshly ground black pepper. Stir through the parsley and serve.

SWEET PAPRIKA VEAL GOULASH

SERVES 4

1 kg (2 lb 4 oz) boneless veal shoulder

1 onion, sliced

2 garlic cloves, crushed

1 tablespoon sweet paprika

½ teaspoon caraway seeds

2 bay leaves

625 g (1 lb 6 oz/2½ cups) tomato
passata (puréed tomatoes)

125 ml (4 fl oz/½ cup) chicken stock

125 ml (4 fl oz/½ cup) red wine

2 all-purpose potatoes, diced

275 g (10 oz) jar roasted red capsicums
(peppers), drained and rinsed

sour cream, to serve

1   Cut the veal into 2.5 cm (1 inch) cubes. Put the veal, onion, garlic, paprika, caraway seeds, bay leaves, tomato passata, stock, wine and potato in the slow cooker. Cook on high for 4 hours, or until the veal is tender. Stir through the capsicum and cook for a further 5 minutes, or until warmed through.

2   Taste and season with salt and freshly ground black pepper. Serve with a dollop of sour cream and with cooked fettuccine noodles.

BRAISED BEEF SHORT RIBS

SERVES 6

2 kg (4 lb 8 oz) beef short ribs

180 g (6½ oz) bacon slices

2 onions, chopped

1 garlic clove, crushed

1 small red chilli, seeded and thinly sliced

500 ml (17 fl oz/2 cups) beef stock

400 g (14 oz) tin chopped tomatoes

8 bulb spring onions (scallions), trimmed and leaves removed

2 strips lemon zest, white pith removed

1 teaspoon mild paprika

1 teaspoon chopped rosemary

1 bay leaf

1 tablespoon soft brown sugar

1 teaspoon worcestershire sauce

2 tablespoons chopped basil

2 tablespoons chopped flat-leaf (Italian) parsley

1 Chop the ribs into 4 cm (1½ inch) lengths. Remove the rind and fat from the bacon and cut into very small dice.

2 Put the ribs, bacon, onion, garlic, chilli, stock, tomato, spring onions, strips of lemon zest, paprika, rosemary, bay leaf, brown sugar and worcestershire sauce in the slow cooker. Cook on high for 4–5 hours, or until the ribs are tender.

3 Skim off as much fat as you can from the top. Stir through the basil and parsley. Serve the ribs with mashed potatoes or soft polenta if desired.

STIFATHO

SERVES 4

1 kg (2 lb 4 oz) chuck steak
500 g (1 lb 2 oz) whole baby onions
1 garlic clove, cut in half lengthways
125 ml (4 fl oz/½ cup) red wine
125 ml (4 fl oz/½ cup) beef stock
1 cinnamon stick
4 whole cloves
1 bay leaf
1 tablespoon red wine vinegar
2 tablespoons tomato paste (concentrated purée)
2 tablespoons currants

1 **Trim the beef** of excess fat and sinew, then cut into 5 cm (2 inch) cubes. Put beef, onions, garlic, wine, stock, cinnamon stick, cloves, bay leaf, vinegar and tomato paste in the slow cooker and season with freshly ground black pepper. Cook on high for 4 hours.

2 **Stir in the currants** and cook a further 15 minutes. Discard cinnamon stick and season to taste with salt and extra pepper. Serve with rice, bread or potatoes.

BRAISED VEAL SHANKS

SERVES 4–6

4–6 veal shanks (about 2 kg/4 lb 8 oz)

200 g (7 oz/1⅔ cups) plain
  (all-purpose) flour

1 leek, white part only, finely diced

1 onion, finely diced

1 carrot, finely diced

1 celery stalk, finely diced

2 garlic cloves, finely chopped

1 bay leaf

1 rosemary sprig, leaves chopped

125 ml (4 fl oz/½ cup) red wine

500 ml (17 fl oz/2 cups) veal stock

200 g (7 oz) artichoke halves

80 g (2¾ oz/½ cup) frozen peas

ORANGE GREMOLATA

1 garlic clove, finely chopped

grated zest of 1 orange

1 small handful flat-leaf (Italian) parsley,
  finely chopped

1 **Coat the veal** shanks in the flour and shake off the excess. Put the veal in the slow cooker along with the leek, onion, carrot, celery, garlic, bay leaf, rosemary, wine and stock. Cook on high for 3 hours.

2 **Add the artichokes** to the slow cooker. Continue to cook on high, with the lid off, for 1 hour. Add the peas and cook for a further 5 minutes, or until the peas are cooked through. Season to taste with salt and freshly ground black pepper.

3 **To make** the orange gremolata, combine the garlic, orange zest and parsley. Serve the veal shanks sprinkled with the gremolata.

VEAL, LEMON AND CAPER CASSEROLE

SERVES 4

300 g (10½ oz) French shallots, unpeeled

1 kg (2 lb 4 oz) boneless veal shoulder

2 garlic cloves, crushed

3 leeks, white part only, cut into large chunks

2 tablespoons plain (all-purpose) flour

500 ml (17 fl oz/2 cups) chicken stock

1 teaspoon grated lemon zest

4 tablespoons lemon juice

2 bay leaves

2 tablespoons capers, rinsed well

chopped flat-leaf (Italian) parsley, to serve

caperberries, to garnish (optional)

1 Put the shallots in a heatproof bowl. Pour over boiling water to cover and set aside for 5 minutes to soften. Drain and peel.

2 Trim veal and cut into 4 cm (1½ inch) cubes. Put shallots and veal cubes in the slow cooker along with the garlic, leek, flour, stock, lemon zest, lemon juice and bay leaves. Stir to combine. Cook on high for 4 hours, or until the veal is tender. During the last 30 minutes of cooking, remove the lid to allow the sauce to reduce a little.

3 To serve, stir in the capers and season with salt and freshly ground black pepper. Sprinkle with parsley and garnish with caperberries if desired.

BEEF OSSO BUCO

SERVES 4

75 g (2½ oz/½ cup) plain (all-purpose) flour

1 kg (2 lb 4 oz) beef osso buco

2–3 tablespoons oil

1 onion, finely chopped

1 carrot, finely chopped

2 bay leaves

½ teaspoon black peppercorns

400 g (14 oz) tin chopped tomatoes

185 ml (6 fl oz/¾ cup) white wine

155 g (5½ oz/1 cup) frozen peas

1 handful flat-leaf (Italian) parsley, chopped

GREMOLATA

2 garlic cloves, finely chopped

1 handful flat-leaf (Italian) parsley, chopped

grated zest of 2 lemons

1 In a flat dish, season the flour with salt and freshly ground black pepper. Dust the osso buco in the seasoned flour.

2 Heat the oil in a large frying pan over medium heat, add the osso buco in batches and cook for about 5 minutes on each side, or until golden brown all over.

3 Put the onion, carrot, bay leaves, peppercorns and osso bucco in the slow cooker and pour over the tomatoes and wine. Cook on high for 5–6 hours, or until the beef is tender. Add the peas and cook for a further 5 minutes.

4 Just before the osso buco is cooked, prepare the gremolata. Combine the garlic, parsley and lemon zest in a bowl, cover and set aside.

5 Before serving, season beef with salt and freshly ground black pepper and stir through the parsley. Transfer to serving plates, then sprinkle with gremolata. Serve with mashed potatoes and steamed vegetables.

BEEF CHEEKS WITH ONIONS, MUSHROOMS AND THYME

SERVES 4

1 kg (2 lb 4 oz) beef cheeks

100 g (3½ oz) bacon or speck, trimmed of fat, chopped

250 ml (9 fl oz/1 cup) red wine

2 celery stalks, finely chopped

1 carrot, finely chopped

1 onion, finely chopped

10 g (¼ oz) thyme

3 garlic cloves

250 ml (9 fl oz/1 cup) beef stock

40 g (1½ oz) butter

12 baby onions, peeled and trimmed, halved lengthways if large

1½ tablespoons sugar

1½ tablespoons sherry vinegar

16 button mushrooms, halved

1 **Trim the beef** cheeks of excess fat and sinew, then cut into four portions. Put beef in the slow cooker along with the bacon, wine, celery, carrot, onion, thyme, garlic and stock. Cook on low for 7 hours (this will vary slightly, depending on the thickness of the beef), or until meat is almost falling apart.

2 **Place half** the butter in a heavy-based frying pan, add the onions and cook over low–medium heat for about 8 minutes, or until golden. Add sugar and cook until caramelized, shaking pan occasionally to ensure that it caramelises evenly. Add half the vinegar and stir to remove any sediment from the bottom of the pan. Transfer to the slow cooker.

3 **Melt remaining butter** in the pan, add the mushrooms and cook over medium heat for 5–6 minutes, or until golden. Pour in the remaining vinegar and stir to remove any sediment from the bottom of the pan.

4 **Add mushrooms** to the slow cooker and cook, uncovered, for a further 1 hour, or until the beef is tender and the sauce has reduced and thickened slightly.

5 **Serve beef cheeks** with the sauce, and with mashed potato and steamed green vegetables.

SICHUAN AND ANISE BEEF STEW

SERVES 6–8

1 kg (2 lb 4 oz) chuck steak

1½ tablespoons plain (all-purpose) flour

1 large red onion, thickly sliced

2 garlic cloves, crushed

3 tablespoons tomato paste
(concentrated purée)

250 ml (9 fl oz/1 cup) red wine

250 ml (9 fl oz/1 cup) beef stock

2 bay leaves, crushed

3 long strips orange zest, about 1.5 cm
(½ in) wide

2 star anise

1 teaspoon sichuan peppercorns

1 teaspoon chopped thyme

1 tablespoon chopped rosemary

3 tablespoons chopped coriander
(cilantro) leaves

1 **Trim the beef** and cut into 2.5 cm (1 inch) cubes. Put beef, flour, onion, garlic, tomato paste, wine, stock, bay leaves, orange zest, star anise, peppercorns, thyme and rosemary in the slow cooker and cook on high for 3 hours, or until the beef is tender.

2 **Season to taste** with salt and freshly ground black pepper. Stir in most of the coriander and garnish with the remainder. Serve the stew with steamed rice.

ZARZUELA

SERVES 6

250 ml (9 fl oz/1 cup) dry white wine

large pinch of saffron threads

3 garlic cloves, thinly sliced

1 leek, white part only, thinly sliced

1 red and 1 green capsicum (pepper)

2 teaspoons paprika

400 g (14 oz) tin chopped tomatoes

20 g (¾ oz) blanched almonds, chopped

1 bay leaf

1 small red chilli, seeded and chopped

3 tablespoons brandy or cognac

2 tablespoons lemon juice

1.5 litres (52 fl oz/6 cups) fish stock

500 g (1 lb 2 oz) skinless white fish fillets

500 g (1 lb 2 oz) small squid tubes

12 mussels and 12 raw prawns (shrimp)

12 fresh clams (vongole) in shell

3 large flat-leaf (Italian) parsley sprigs

ROMESCO SAUCE

80 g (2¾ oz/½ cup) blanched almonds

285 g (10 oz) jar roasted red capsicums
(peppers), drained and rinsed

2 teaspoons sweet paprika

2 slices stale white bread

2 garlic cloves, roughly chopped

2 tablespoons sherry vinegar

125 ml (4 fl oz/½ cup) olive oil

1 **Combine the wine,** saffron, garlic, leek, red and green capsicum (seeded and thinly sliced), paprika, tomatoes, almonds, bay leaf, chilli, brandy, lemon juice and stock in the slow cooker. Cook on high for 3 hours.

2 **Prepare the seafood.** Cut the fish into 2.5 cm (1 inch) cubes. Clean the squid tubes and cut into rings. Scrub the mussels and clams with a stiff brush. Pull out the hairy beards from the mussels. Discard any broken mussels or clams or open ones that don't close when tapped on the work surface. Peel the prawns, leaving the tails intact. Gently pull out the dark vein from each prawn back, starting at the head end.

3 **Add the prepared seafood** and parsley to the slow cooker and cook for a further 30 minutes, or until seafood is cooked and the mussels and clams have opened. Discard any that remain closed. Remove the parsley from the soup.

4 **To make the romesco sauce,** place the almonds, roasted capsicum, paprika, bread (torn into large pieces), garlic and vinegar in the bowl of a food processor. Process until smooth, then gradually add enough of the olive oil until you have a thick sauce.

5 **Stir enough** of the romesco sauce through the zarzuela to thicken it slightly. Divide among serving bowls and top with the remaining sauce. Serve with crusty bread.

BASQUE CHICKEN

SERVES 4

1.8 kg (4 lb) chicken

1 onion, cut into small dice

1 red capsicum (pepper), cut into small dice

1 green capsicum (pepper), cut into small dice

2 garlic cloves, finely chopped

200 g (7 oz) chorizo sausage, sliced

150 ml (5 fl oz) white wine

80 g (2¾ oz) tomato paste (concentrated purée)

90 g (3¼ oz/½ cup) black olives

¼ preserved lemon or small piece of lemon peel

2 tablespoons chopped basil

2 tablespoons chopped flat-leaf (Italian) parsley

1 Joint the chicken into eight pieces by removing both legs and cutting between the joint of the drumstick and the thigh. Cut down either side of the backbone and lift it out. Turn the chicken over and cut through the cartilage down the centre of the breastbone. Cut each breast in half, leaving the wing attached to the top half.

2 Combine the chicken pieces, onion, red and green capsicum, garlic, chorizo, wine, tomato paste and olives in the slow cooker.

3 Rinse the preserved lemon well, remove and discard the pulp and membrane and finely dice the rind. Add to the chicken and cook on low for 8 hours, or until cooked through.

4 Stir in the basil and serve sprinkled with the parsley. Serve with rice if desired.

CHICKEN AGRODOLCE

SERVES 6

1.2 kg (2 lb 10 oz) chicken pieces, skin removed

1 garlic clove

1 tablespoon dried oregano

2 bay leaves

125 ml (4 fl oz/½ cup) red wine vinegar

125 ml (4 fl oz/½ cup) dry white wine

3 tablespoons soft brown sugar

220 g (7¾ oz/1 cup) pitted prunes

2 tablespoons capers, rinsed

175 g (6 oz/1 cup) green olives

1 handful flat-leaf (Italian) parsley, chopped

1 **Combine the chicken**, garlic, oregano, bay leaves, vinegar, wine and brown sugar in the slow cooker and cook on low for 3 hours.

2 **Stir in the prunes**, capers and olives and cook for a further 30 minutes, or until the chicken is cooked through. Season with salt and freshly ground black pepper and stir through the parsley. Serve with mashed potato.

PORK BELLY WITH VEGETABLES AND LENTILS

SERVES 6

1 kg (2 lb 4 oz) pork belly

1 onion

4 cloves

1 large carrot, cut into chunks

200 g (7 oz) swede (rutabaga) or turnips, cut into chunks

100 g (3½ oz) leek, white part only, thickly sliced

1 parsnip, cut into chunks

1 garlic clove

1 bouquet garni (see Note on page 31)

2 bay leaves

6 juniper berries, slightly crushed

350 g (12 oz/1¾ cups) puy lentils or tiny blue-green lentils

2 tablespoons chopped flat-leaf (Italian) parsley

1   **Slice the pork** belly into thick strips. Stud the onion with the cloves. Put the pork strips in the slow cooker along with the studded onion and all the remaining ingredients except the lentils and parsley. Stir thoroughly, then add just enough water to half cover the ingredients. Cook on high for 4 hours.

2   **Put the lentils** in a sieve and rinse under cold running water. Add to the slow cooker and cook for a further 1 hour, or until the pork and lentils are tender and cooked through.

3   **Drain the mixture** into a colander, discarding the liquid. Place the contents of the colander in a serving dish, except for the onion, which can be discarded.

4   **Season the pork** and lentils with plenty of freshly ground black pepper and taste to see if you need any salt. Just before serving, stir in the chopped parsley.

SPANISH-STYLE PORK AND VEGETABLE STEW

SERVES 4–6

1 kg (2 lb 4 oz) boneless pork shoulder

2 spicy chorizo sausages, sliced

600 g (1 lb 5 oz) all-purpose potatoes, cubed

1 red onion, diced

2 garlic cloves, chopped

2 red capsicums (peppers), seeded and chopped

400 g (14 oz) tin chopped tomatoes

pinch of saffron threads

1 tablespoon sweet paprika

10 large thyme sprigs

1 bay leaf

3 tablespoons tomato paste (concentrated purée)

125 ml (4 fl oz/½ cup) white wine

125 ml (4 fl oz/½ cup) chicken stock

2 tablespoons sherry

1 handful flat-leaf (Italian) parsley, chopped

1 Trim the pork and cut into 4 cm (1½ inch) cubes. Put the pork, chorizo, potato, onion, garlic, capsicum, tomato, saffron, paprika, thyme and bay leaf in the slow cooker.

2 Combine tomato paste, wine, stock and sherry in a small bowl and pour over the pork and vegetables. Cook on high for 4 hours, or until the pork is tender.

3 Season to taste with salt and freshly ground black pepper. Stir through the parsley and serve.

ITALIAN BEEF CASSEROLE WITH DUMPLINGS

SERVES 4–6

1 kg (2 lb 4 oz) chuck, blade or skirt steak

1 onion, sliced

2 garlic cloves, crushed

250 ml (9 fl oz/1 cup) beef stock

2 x 425 g (15 oz) tins chopped tomatoes

450 g (1 lb) jar roasted red capsicums (peppers), drained and thickly sliced

1 tablespoon chopped oregano

90 g (3¼ oz/⅓ cup) ready-made pesto, to serve

DUMPLINGS

4 tablespoons plain (all-purpose) flour

3 tablespoons polenta

1 teaspoon baking powder

1 egg white

2 tablespoons milk

1 tablespoon olive oil

1 **Trim the beef** and cut into 3 cm (1¼ inch) cubes. Put the beef cubes, onion, garlic, stock, tomato, capsicum and oregano in the slow cooker. Season with salt and freshly ground black pepper. Cook on high for 4 hours, or until the beef is tender.

2 **To make dumplings,** combine the flour, polenta, baking powder and ½ teaspoon salt in a large bowl. Make a well in the centre and add the egg white, milk and olive oil. Stir well to combine. Using teaspoonfuls of the polenta mixture, form it into small balls. Add the dumplings to the slow cooker and cook for a further 30 minutes, or until the dumplings are cooked through.

3 **Check the seasoning** and add extra salt and pepper if needed. Serve the casserole and dumplings topped with a dollop of pesto.

ITALIAN MEATBALLS WITH TOMATO SAUCE

SERVES 4–6

MEATBALLS

1 onion, finely chopped

80 g (2¾ oz/½ cup) pine nuts, roughly chopped

2 garlic cloves, crushed

1 small handful flat-leaf (Italian) parsley, roughly chopped

1 teaspoon chopped rosemary

2 teaspoons fennel seeds, ground

4 tablespoons fresh breadcrumbs

3 tablespoons grated parmesan cheese

grated zest of 1 large lemon

1 egg

500 g (1 lb 2 oz) minced (ground) pork or beef

700 g (1 lb 9 oz) tomato passata (puréed tomatoes)

125 ml (4 fl oz/½ cup) red wine

1 To make the meatballs, combine all the ingredients in a bowl. Use your hands to mix well. Roll the mixture into walnut-sized balls and place on a tray. Refrigerate the meatballs for 20 minutes.

2 Put the tomato passata, wine and meatballs in the slow cooker. Season with salt and freshly ground black pepper and cook on high for 4 hours, or until the meatballs are cooked through and tender.

3 Serve the meatballs and tomato sauce with spaghetti, rice or mashed potatoes, and a side salad.

GREEK LAMB WITH MACARONI

SERVES 4–6

1 kg (2 lb 4 oz) boneless lamb leg

1 large onion, chopped

2 garlic cloves, crushed

400 g (14 oz) tin chopped tomatoes

3 tablespoons tomato paste
   (concentrated purée)

500 ml (17 fl oz/2 cups) beef stock

2 tablespoons red wine vinegar

1 tablespoon soft brown sugar

1 teaspoon dried oregano

200 g (7 oz/1½ cups) macaroni pasta

125 g (4½ oz) pecorino cheese, grated

1   Trim the lamb of any excess fat and cut into 3 cm (1 in) cubes. Put the lamb, onion, garlic, tomato, tomato paste, stock, vinegar, brown sugar and oregano in the slow cooker. Cook on high for 1¾ hours, or until the lamb is tender.

2   Place the macaroni in a large heatproof bowl and cover with boiling water. Set aside for 10 minutes. Drain and add the macaroni to the slow cooker and stir to combine. Cook for a further 30 minutes, or until the pasta is tender and the liquid has absorbed.

3   Divide among serving bowls and sprinkle with cheese.

VEAL OLIVES WITH PROSCIUTTO, CHEESE AND SAGE

SERVES 4

TOMATO AND OLIVE SAUCE

400 g (14 oz) tin chopped tomatoes
2 semi-dried (sun-blushed) tomatoes, chopped
2 spring onions (scallions), chopped
2 garlic cloves, crushed
10 black olives, pitted and chopped
1 teaspoon caster (superfine) sugar

6 x 150 g (5½ oz) veal leg steaks (schnitzel)
6 prosciutto slices, trimmed of fat
50 g (1¾ oz/½ cup) grated parmesan cheese
finely grated zest of 1 lemon
12 sage leaves
1 tablespoon olive oil
20 g (¾ oz) butter
1 tablespoon cornflour (cornstarch) (optional)
extra sage leaves, to garnish

1 To make the tomato and olive sauce, combine the tomato, semi-dried tomatoes, spring onion, garlic, olives and sugar in a bowl. Season with salt and freshly ground black pepper. Pour half the tomato sauce into the slow cooker and set the remainder aside.

2 Put each veal steak between two sheets of plastic wrap and use the flat side of a meat mallet to pound them to about 5 mm (¼ inch) thick and roughly 25 x 10 cm (10 x 4 inches) in size.

3 Lay the prosciutto slices along the top of each veal steak. Evenly divide the parmesan, lemon zest and sage leaves along each veal steak. Season with freshly ground black pepper. Roll up the veal and secure with a toothpick to form veal olives.

4 Heat the oil and butter in a large frying pan. When the oil is hot, add the veal olives and cook for 5 minutes, turning frequently until browned. Arrange the veal olives over the tomato sauce in the slow cooker. They will be packed in side by side. Pour over the remaining tomato sauce. Cook on low for 6–8 hours, or until the veal is tender. Remove the veal olives to a side plate and remove the toothpicks, cover and keep warm.

5 If you like, you can thicken the sauce. Combine the cornflour in a bowl with 1 tablespoon water until smooth, then stir into the sauce. Stir over high heat until thickened.

6 To serve, cut each veal olive into three or four thick slices diagonally and arrange onto serving plates. Pour over the sauce and garnish with an extra sage leaf or two. Serve with mashed potato or polenta and a green vegetable or salad.

VEAL WITH PEPERONATA AND GNOCCHI

SERVES 4

PEPERONATA

400 g (14 oz) tin whole tomatoes

1 red onion, cut into thin wedges

2 garlic cloves, chopped

1 red or green chilli, seeded and finely
   chopped (optional)

1 red capsicum (pepper), seeded and
   thinly sliced

1 yellow capsicum (pepper), seeded and
   thinly sliced

1 tablespoon red wine vinegar

1 teaspoon caster (superfine) sugar

60 g (2 oz/½ cup) plain (all-purpose)
   flour

4 even-sized pieces (about 750 g/
   1 lb 10 oz) veal osso bucco

20 g (¾ oz) butter

1 tablespoon olive oil

125 ml (4 fl oz/½ cup) white wine

350 g (12 oz) packet potato gnocchi

GREMOLATA

grated zest of 1 lemon

1 garlic clove, finely chopped

1 large handful flat-leaf (Italian) parsley,
   finely chopped

1 To make the peperonata, put the tomatoes in a large
bowl and roughly chop with scissors or a knife. Add the
remaining peperonata ingredients and mix to combine. Season
with salt and freshly ground black pepper. Add half of the
peperonata to the slow cooker.

2 Put the flour in a flat dish and season well with salt and
freshly ground black pepper. Trim the osso bucco pieces of
excess fat and then coat the veal in the seasoned flour.

3 Heat the butter and oil in a large frying pan over medium
heat. When the oil is hot, add the osso bucco and brown
well for 2–3 minutes on each side. Pour in the wine and let
it bubble and reduce a little. Arrange the browned veal in
a single layer on top of the peperonata in the slow cooker.
Pour in any juices left in the frying pan, then spoon over the
remaining peperonata.

4 Cook on high for 4–6 hours, or until the veal is very
tender. Remove the osso bucco to a side plate, cover and keep
warm. Add the gnocchi to the peperonata in the slow cooker
and stir to combine. Cover and cook for a further 20 minutes,
or until the gnocchi is tender.

5 To make the gremolata, combine the lemon zest, garlic
and parsley in a small bowl.

6 To serve, spoon the gnocchi and peperonata onto
serving plates, top with the osso bucco and sprinkle over
the gremolata.

PROSCIUTTO WRAPPED BEEF WITH BROAD BEANS

SERVES 4

500 g (1 lb 2 oz) thick beef fillet

3 garlic cloves, thinly sliced

2 tablespoons chopped rosemary

8–10 thin slices prosciutto, pancetta or smoked bacon

2 tablespoons olive oil

20 g (¾ oz) dried wild mushrooms, such as porcini

1 onion, halved and sliced

170 ml (5½ fl oz) red wine

400 g (14 oz) tin chopped tomatoes

400 g (14 oz) peeled broad (fava) beans

1 Trim the beef of excess fat. Make several small incisions around the beef and push a slice of garlic into each incision, using up one of the garlic cloves. Sprinkle 1 tablespoon of the rosemary over the beef and season with salt and freshly ground black pepper.

2 Lay the prosciutto slices on a board in a line next to each other, creating a sheet of prosciutto to wrap the beef in. Place the beef fillet across them and fold the prosciutto over to enclose the beef. Tie several times with kitchen string to keep the beef and prosciutto together. Leave in the refrigerator to rest for at least 15 minutes.

3 Heat the olive oil in a large frying pan over high heat. Add the beef and sear on all sides until the prosciutto is golden brown, but not burnt. A little of the prosciutto might fall off, but it doesn't matter: just make sure the beef is well sealed. Remove from the pan.

4 Put the dried mushrooms in a bowl with 185 ml (6 fl oz/ ¾ cup) hot water and soak for 10 minutes.

5 Put the beef in the slow cooker along with the onion, remaining garlic and rosemary, the mushrooms and soaking liquid, wine and tomatoes. Cook on low for 2 hours, or until the beef is tender.

6 Add the broad beans and cook for a further 20 minutes. Season with salt and freshly ground black pepper and serve with mashed potato or soft polenta.

TAGINES

LAMB TAGINE WITH PEAS AND LEMONS

SERVES 4–6

1 kg (2 lb 4 oz) lamb shoulder or leg, boned

2 tablespoons olive oil

1 onion, finely chopped

2 garlic cloves, finely chopped

1 teaspoon ground cumin

½ teaspoon ground ginger

½ teaspoon ground turmeric

3 tablespoons chopped coriander (cilantro) leaves

3 tablespoons chopped flat-leaf (Italian) parsley

2 teaspoons chopped lemon thyme

1½ preserved lemons (see Note)

235 g (8½ oz/1½ cups) peas

2 teaspoons chopped mint

½ teaspoon sugar

1 **Trim the lamb** and cut into 3 cm (1¼ inch) pieces. Heat the oil in a large saucepan over high heat and brown the lamb, in batches, removing to a dish when cooked. Add more oil if required.

2 **Reduce the heat** to low, add the onion and cook for 5 minutes, or until softened. Add the garlic, cumin, ginger and turmeric and cook for a few seconds. Add 375 ml (13 fl oz/ 1½ cups) water and stir well to lift the browned juices off the base of the pan, then return the lamb to the pan with a little salt and a good grinding of black pepper. Add the coriander, parsley and thyme, cover and simmer over low heat for 1½ hours, or until the lamb is tender.

3 **Separate the preserved lemons** into quarters and rinse well under cold running water, removing and discarding the pulp. Cut the rind into strips and add to the lamb, along with the peas, mint and sugar. Return to a simmer, cover and simmer for a further 10 minutes, or until the peas are cooked. Serve hot.

Note: Preserved lemons are available in jars from Middle Eastern supermarkets and delicatessens. They give this dish its distinctive taste. If you can't find them, use the rind of 1 large lemon, removing as much pith as possible.

SPICED LENTIL AND PUMPKIN TAGINE

SERVES 4–6

275 g (9¾ oz/1½ cups) brown lentils

2 tomatoes

600 g (1 lb 5 oz) firm pumpkin (winter squash) or butternut pumpkin (squash)

3 tablespoons olive oil

1 onion, finely chopped

3 garlic cloves, finely chopped

½ teaspoon ground cumin

½ teaspoon ground turmeric

⅛ teaspoon cayenne pepper (or 1 teaspoon harissa, or to taste)

1 teaspoon paprika

3 teaspoons tomato paste (concentrated purée)

½ teaspoon sugar

1 teaspoon salt

1 tablespoon finely chopped flat-leaf (Italian) parsley

2 tablespoons chopped coriander (cilantro) leaves

1 Rinse the lentils in a sieve. Tip into a saucepan and add 1 litre (35 fl oz/4 cups) cold water. Bring to the boil, skim the surface, if necessary, then cover and simmer over low heat for 20 minutes.

2 Halve the tomatoes horizontally and squeeze out the seeds. Coarsely grate the tomatoes into a bowl down to the skin, discarding the skin. Set the tomato aside. Peel and seed the pumpkin and cut into 3 cm (1¼ inch) dice. Set aside.

3 Heat the oil in a large saucepan, add the onion and cook over low heat until softened. Add the garlic, cook for a few seconds, then stir in the cumin, turmeric and cayenne pepper or harissa. Cook for 30 seconds, then add the grated tomatoes, paprika, tomato paste, sugar, salt, half the parsley and coriander, and freshly ground black pepper, to taste. Add the drained lentils and chopped pumpkin, stir well, then cover and simmer for 20 minutes, or until the pumpkin and lentils are tender. Adjust the seasoning and sprinkle with the remaining parsley and coriander. Serve hot or warm with crusty bread.

LAMB TAGINE WITH SWEET TOMATO JAM

SERVES 4–6

2 tablespoons olive oil

1 kg (2 lb 4 oz) lamb shoulder or leg steaks, trimmed and cut into 3 cm (1¼ inch) thick pieces

2 onions, coarsely grated

1.5 kg (3 lb 5 oz) ripe tomatoes, halved horizontally

2 garlic cloves, finely chopped

1 teaspoon ground ginger

¼ teaspoon freshly ground black pepper

1 cinnamon stick

3 tablespoons tomato paste (concentrated purée)

⅛ teaspoon ground saffron threads (optional)

30 g (1 oz) butter

3 tablespoons blanched almonds

2 tablespoons honey

1½ teaspoons ground cinnamon

1 Heat half the oil in a heavy-based saucepan over high heat and brown the lamb, in batches. Remove and set aside. Reduce the heat to low, add the remaining oil and the onion and cook gently, stirring occasionally, for 10 minutes, or until the onion is softened.

2 Squeeze out the tomato seeds. Coarsely grate the tomatoes down to the skin, discarding the skin. Stir the garlic, ginger, pepper and cinnamon into the pan and cook for 1 minute. Add the tomato paste and saffron, if using, and cook for 1 minute. Return the lamb to the pan, stir in the grated tomato and season.

3 Cover and simmer gently for 1¼ hours. Simmer, partly covered, for 15 minutes, stirring occasionally, then simmer, uncovered, for 25 minutes, or until the sauce has thickened and has an almost jam-like consistency with the oil beginning to separate.

4 Melt the butter in a small frying pan, add the almonds and cook over medium heat, stirring occasionally, until golden. Stir the honey and cinnamon into the tagine and simmer for 2 minutes. Serve with couscous, sprinkled with the almonds.

LAMB SHANK AND PRUNE TAGINE

SERVES 4

1 tablespoon oil

30 g (1 oz) butter

4 frenched lamb shanks (see Note)

1 onion, chopped

¼ teaspoon ground saffron threads

½ teaspoon ground ginger

2 cinnamon sticks

4 coriander (cilantro) sprigs, tied in
 a bunch

½ lemon, zest removed in wide strips

300 g (10½ oz/1⅓ cups) pitted prunes

2 tablespoons honey

1 tablespoon sesame seeds, toasted

1 Place a heavy-based saucepan over high heat, add the oil and butter, then add the lamb shanks. Brown the shanks on all sides and remove to a plate. Reduce the heat to medium, add the onion and cook gently for 5 minutes to soften. Add 375 ml (13 fl oz/1½ cups) water, the saffron threads, ginger, cinnamon sticks and coriander (cilantro) sprigs. Season to taste.

2 Stir well and return the lamb shanks to the pan. Cover and simmer over low heat for 1 hour. Add the lemon to the pan and cook for a further 30 minutes. Add the prunes and honey, cover and simmer for a further 30 minutes until the lamb is very tender. Remove and discard the coriander sprigs. Serve hot, sprinkled with the sesame seeds.

Note: Frenched lamb shanks are trimmed of excess fat with the knuckle end of the bone sawn off. If unavailable, use whole shanks and ask the butcher to saw them in half for you.

BEEF TAGINE WITH SWEET POTATOES

SERVES 4–6

1 kg (2 lb 4 oz) blade or chuck steak

3 tablespoons olive oil

1 onion, finely chopped

½ teaspoon cayenne pepper

½ teaspoon ground cumin

1 teaspoon ground turmeric

½ teaspoon ground ginger

2 teaspoons paprika

1 teaspoon salt

2 tablespoons chopped flat-leaf (Italian) parsley

2 tablespoons chopped coriander (cilantro) leaves

2 tomatoes, peeled and sliced

500 g (1 lb 2 oz) orange sweet potatoes

1 **Trim the steak** of any fat and cut into 2.5 cm (1 inch) pieces. Heat half the oil in a saucepan and brown the beef in batches over high heat, adding more oil as needed. Set aside in a dish.

2 **Reduce the heat** to low, add the onion and the remaining oil to the pan and gently cook for 10 minutes, or until the onion is softened. Add the cayenne pepper, cumin, turmeric, ginger and paprika, cook for a few seconds, then add the salt and a good grinding of black pepper. Return beef to the pan, add the parsley, coriander and 250 ml (9 fl oz/1 cup) water. Cover and simmer over low heat for 1½ hours, or until the meat is almost tender.

3 **Peel the sweet potatoes**, cut them into 2 cm (¾ inch) dice and leave in cold water until required, as this will prevent them from discolouring. Preheat the oven to 180°C (350°F/Gas 4).

4 **Transfer the meat** and its sauce to an ovenproof serving dish (the base of a tagine would be ideal). Drain the sweet potato and spread it on top of the beef. Top with the tomato slices. Cover with foil (or the lid of the tagine) and bake for 40 minutes. Remove the foil, increase the oven temperature to 220°C (425°F/Gas 7) and raise the dish to the upper oven shelf. Cook until the tomato and sweet potato are flecked with brown and are tender. Serve from the dish.

TAGINE OF CHICKPEAS

SERVES 4

3 tablespoons olive oil

1 brown onion, chopped

1 garlic clove, finely chopped

1 teaspoon harissa, or to taste, or
¼ teaspoon cayenne pepper

½ teaspoon paprika

¼ teaspoon ground ginger

½ teaspoon ground turmeric

1 teaspoon ground cumin

1 teaspoon ground cinnamon

400 g (14 oz) tin chopped tomatoes

1 teaspoon caster (superfine) sugar

2 x 420 g (15 oz) tins chickpeas

3 tablespoons chopped flat-leaf (Italian)
parsley

2 tablespoons chopped coriander
(cilantro) leaves

1 Put the olive oil and onion in a large saucepan and cook over medium heat for 7–8 minutes, or until softened. Stir in the garlic, the harissa or cayenne pepper, and the spices and cook gently for 2 minutes or until fragrant. Add the tomatoes and sugar and season, to taste. Cover and simmer for 20 minutes.

2 Meanwhile, drain the chickpeas and put them in a large bowl with enough cold water to cover well. Lift up handfuls of chickpeas and rub them between your hands to loosen the skins. Run more water into the bowl, stir well and let the skins float to the top, then skim them off. Repeat until all the skins have been removed.

3 Drain the chickpeas again and stir them into the tomato mixture. Cover and simmer for 20–25 minutes, adding a little more water if necessary. Stir through the parsley and coriander and season, to taste. Serve with crusty bread or with couscous.

TAGINE OF BEEF WITH APPLES AND RAISINS

SERVES 6

1 kg (2 lb 4 oz) chuck or blade steak

2 tablespoons oil

40 g (1½ oz) butter

1 onion, sliced

¼ teaspoon ground saffron threads

½ teaspoon ground ginger

1 teaspoon ground cinnamon, plus
 ½ teaspoon extra

1½ teaspoons salt

4 sprigs coriander (cilantro), tied in
 a bunch

125 g (4½ oz/1 cup) raisins

3 tablespoons honey

3 tart Granny Smiths apples, halved,
 cored and cut into thick wedges

1 tablespoon sesame seeds, toasted

1 Trim the beef and cut it into 2.5 cm (1 inch) cubes. Heat half the oil and half the butter in a heavy-based saucepan over a high heat and brown the beef in batches. Remove to a dish when cooked. Add the remaining oil as needed, and set aside the remaining butter.

2 Reduce the heat to medium, add the onion and cook for 5 minutes to soften. Add the saffron, ginger and cinnamon and cook for 1 minute. Stir in 375 ml (13 fl oz/1½ cups) water, the salt and a generous grinding of black pepper. Return the beef to the pan, along with the coriander. Cover and simmer over low heat for 1½ hours. Add the raisins and 1 tablespoon of the honey, cover and simmer for a further 30 minutes, or until the meat is tender.

3 Heat remaining butter in a frying pan and cook the apple for 10 minutes, turning often. Drizzle with the remaining honey, dust with the extra cinnamon and cook for 5 minutes, or until glazed and softened. Transfer the meat and sauce to a serving dish, arrange the apple on top and sprinkle with the sesame seeds.

MEATBALL TAGINE WITH HERBS AND LEMON

SERVES 4

½ onion, roughly chopped

2 tablespoons roughly chopped flat-leaf (Italian) parsley

2 white bread slices, crusts removed

1 egg

500 g (1 lb 2 oz) minced (ground) lamb or beef

½ teaspoon ground cumin

½ teaspoon paprika

½ teaspoon freshly ground black pepper

HERB AND LEMON SAUCE

1 tablespoon butter or oil

½ onion, finely chopped

½ teaspoon paprika

½ teaspoon ground turmeric

¼ teaspoon ground cumin

1 red chilli, seeded and sliced (or ¼ teaspoon cayenne pepper)

375 ml (13 fl oz/1½ cups) chicken stock

2 tablespoons chopped coriander (cilantro) leaves

2 tablespoons chopped flat-leaf (Italian) parsley

2 tablespoons lemon juice

½ preserved lemon (optional)

1 Put the onion and parsley in a food processor and process until finely chopped. Tear the bread into pieces, add to the onion, along with the egg and process briefly. Add the lamb or beef, cumin, paprika, pepper and 1 teaspoon salt and process to a thick paste, scraping down the side of the bowl occasionally. Alternatively, grate the onion, chop the parsley, crumb the bread and add to the meat in a bowl with the egg, spices and seasoning. Knead until paste-like in consistency.

2 With moistened hands, shape the mixture into walnut-sized balls and place them on a tray. Cover and refrigerate until required.

3 To make the herb and lemon sauce, heat the butter or oil in a saucepan and add the onion. Cook over low heat until softened and golden, then add the paprika, turmeric, cumin and chilli or cayenne pepper and cook, stirring, for 1 minute. Add the chicken stock and coriander and bring to the boil.

4 Add the meatballs to the pan, shaking so that they settle into the sauce. Cover and simmer for 45 minutes. Add most of the parsley and the lemon juice and season, if necessary. Return to the boil and simmer for 2 minutes. If using preserved lemon, rinse well under running water, remove and discard the pulp and cut rind into strips. Add to the meatballs. Transfer to a tagine or bowl and scatter with the remaining parsley. Serve hot with crusty bread.

TAGINE OF LAMB, OLIVES AND POTATOES

SERVES 4–6

1 kg (2 lb 4 oz) boneless lamb shoulder

4 tablespoons olive oil

2 onions, finely chopped

2 garlic cloves, finely chopped

1 teaspoon ground cumin

½ teaspoon ground ginger

½ teaspoon paprika

½ teaspoon salt

3 tablespoons chopped coriander (cilantro) leaves

3 tablespoons chopped flat-leaf (Italian) parsley

175 g (6 oz/1 cup) green olives

750 g (1 lb 10 oz) potatoes

¼ teaspoon ground saffron threads

1 **Trim the lamb** and cut it into 3 cm (1¼ inch) thick pieces. Heat 1½ tablespoons of the olive oil in a large saucepan over high heat and brown the lamb on each side, in batches, removing to a dish when done. Add more oil as required.

2 **Reduce the heat** to low, add another 1½ tablespoons of olive oil and cook the onion for 5 minutes, or until softened. Add the garlic, cumin and ginger and cook for a few seconds. Add 375 ml (13 fl oz/1½ cups) water and stir well to lift the browned juices off the base of the pan. Return the lamb to the pan, along with the paprika, salt and a good grinding of black pepper. Add the coriander and parsley, then cover and simmer over low heat for 1–1¼ hours.

3 **Put the olives** in a small saucepan, cover with water, then bring to the boil and cook for 5 minutes. Drain and repeat once more to sweeten the flavour. Add the drained olives to the lamb, cover and cook for a further 15–30 minutes, or until the lamb is tender.

4 **Peel the potatoes** and cut them into quarters. Put in a pan, cover with lightly salted water and add the saffron. Bring to the boil and cook for 10 minutes, or until tender. Drain and toss lightly with the remaining olive oil.

5 **Transfer the lamb** and sauce to a serving dish, arrange the potatoes around the lamb and serve.

LAMB TAGINE WITH DATES

SERVES 6

1 kg (2 lb 4 oz) boneless lamb from shoulder or leg
30 g (1 oz) butter, plus 15 g (½ oz) extra
1 onion, finely chopped
1 teaspoon ground ginger
1 teaspoon ground cinnamon
½ teaspoon freshly ground black pepper
4 tablespoons pitted and chopped dried dates
a pinch of ground saffron threads
1 teaspoons salt, or to taste
2 tablespoons honey
2 tablespoons lemon juice
200 g (7 oz/1 cup) unpitted fresh or dessert dates
½ preserved lemon
4 tablespoons slivered almonds

1 **Trim lamb** and cut it into 2.5 cm (1 inch) cubes. In a large heavy-based saucepan, melt butter over low heat, add onion and cook gently until softened. Sprinkle in the ground ginger, cinnamon and black pepper and stir for 1 minute. Increase the heat to high, add the lamb and stir until the colour of the meat changes. Reduce heat, add 375 ml (13 fl oz/1½ cups) water, the chopped dates, saffron and salt. Reduce the heat to low, cover and simmer for 1½ hours, stirring occasionally to prevent the sauce sticking as the chopped dates cook to a purée.

2 **Stir in the honey** and lemon juice and adjust seasoning. Place unpitted dates on top, cover and simmer for 10 minutes, or until the dates are plump.

3 **Rinse preserved lemon** under cold running water, remove and discard the pulp. Drain the rind, pat dry with paper towels and cut into strips. Melt the extra butter in a small frying pan, add almonds and brown lightly, stirring often. Tip immediately onto a plate to prevent overbrowning.

4 **Remove the whole dates** from the top of the lamb and set them aside with the almonds. Ladle meat into a serving dish or tagine and scatter the dates on top, along with the lemon strips and roasted almonds. Serve hot.

KEFTA TAGINE

SERVES 4

700 g (1 lb 9 oz) minced (ground) lamb

1 small onion, finely chopped

2 garlic cloves, finely chopped

2 tablespoons finely chopped flat-leaf (Italian) parsley

2 tablespoons finely chopped coriander (cilantro) leaves

½ teaspoon cayenne pepper

½ teaspoon ground ginger

1 teaspoon ground cumin

1 teaspoon paprika

2 tablespoons oil

SAUCE

2 tablespoons olive oil

1 onion, finely chopped

2 garlic cloves, finely chopped

2 teaspoons ground cumin

½ teaspoon ground cinnamon

1 teaspoon paprika

800 g (1 lb 12 oz) tin chopped tomatoes

2 teaspoons harissa, or to taste

4 tablespoons chopped coriander (cilantro) leaves

4 eggs

1 Put the lamb, onion, garlic, herbs and spices in a bowl and mix well. Season with salt and freshly ground black pepper. Roll tablespoons of the mixture into balls.

2 Heat the oil in a large lidded frying pan over medium to high heat, add the meatballs in batches and cook, turning occasionally, for 8–10 minutes, or until browned all over. Remove the meatballs and set aside in a bowl. Wipe the frying pan with paper towels.

3 To make the sauce, heat the olive oil in the frying pan, add the onion and cook over medium heat for 5 minutes, or until the onion is soft. Add the garlic, cumin, cinnamon and paprika and cook for 1 minute, or until fragrant. Stir in the tomato and harissa and bring to the boil. Reduce the heat and simmer for 20 minutes.

4 Add the meatballs, cover and simmer for 10 minutes, or until cooked. Stir in the coriander, then carefully break the eggs into the simmering tagine and cook until just set. (Alternatively, transfer the meatballs and sauce to a large shallow ovenproof serving dish. Add the eggs and cook in a preheated 200°C/400°F/Gas 6 oven for 5–8 minutes, or until the eggs are set.) Season and serve with crusty bread to mop up the juices.

SERVES 4–6

60 g (2¼ oz) butter

1 large onion, finely chopped

2 garlic cloves, finely chopped

1 teaspoon ground ginger

1 teaspoon ground turmeric

1 cinnamon stick

a pinch of cayenne pepper

500 ml (17 fl oz/2 cups) vegetable or
  chicken stock

⅛ teaspoon ground saffron threads

600 g (1 lb 5 oz) butternut pumpkin
  (squash) or other firm pumpkin
  (winter squash), peeled and cubed

500 g (1 lb 2 oz) orange sweet potato,
  peeled and cubed

60 g (2¼ oz/½ cup) raisins

1 tablespoon honey

coriander (cilantro) leaves

1   Melt the butter in a large saucepan over low heat. Add the onion and cook gently, stirring occasionally, until softened. Add the garlic, ground ginger and turmeric, cinnamon stick and cayenne pepper. Stir over low heat for 1–2 minutes

2   Pour in the stock, add the saffron, then increase the heat to medium and bring to the boil. Add pumpkin, sweet potato, raisins and honey and season with salt and freshly ground black pepper.

3   Cover and simmer for a further 15 minutes, or until the vegetables are tender. Remove the cinnamon stick, transfer the tagine to a bowl and scatter with coriander. Serve with couscous or as an accompaniment.

CURRIES

PORK VINDALOO

SERVES 4

1 kg (2 lb 4 oz) leg of pork on the bone, trimmed of excess fat

6 cardamom pods

1 teaspoon black peppercorns

4 dried chillies

1 teaspoon cloves

10 cm (4 inch) piece of cinnamon stick, roughly broken

1 teaspoon cumin seeds

½ teaspoon ground turmeric

½ teaspoon coriander seeds

¼ teaspoon fenugreek seeds

4 tablespoons clear vinegar (see Note)

1 tablespoon dark vinegar (see Note)

4 tablespoons oil

2 onions, finely sliced

10 garlic cloves, finely sliced

5 cm (2 in) piece of ginger, cut into matchsticks

3 ripe tomatoes, roughly chopped

4 green chillies, chopped

1 teaspoon palm sugar (jaggery) or soft brown sugar

1 Remove the bone from the pork and cut the meat into 2.5 cm (1 inch) cubes. Reserve the bone.

2 Split open the cardamom pods and remove the seeds. Finely grind the cardamom seeds and all the other spices in a spice grinder or mortar and pestle. In a large bowl, mix the ground spices with the vinegars. Add the pork and mix thoroughly to coat well. Cover and marinate in the fridge for 3 hours.

3 Heat the oil in a flameproof casserole dish over low heat and fry the onion until lightly browned. Add the garlic, ginger, tomato and chilli and stir well. Add the pork, increase the heat to high and fry for 3–5 minutes, or until browned. Add 250 ml (9 fl oz/1 cup) water and any of the marinade liquid left in the bowl, reduce the heat and bring slowly back to the boil. Add the jaggery and the pork bone. Cover tightly and simmer for 1½ hours, stirring occasionally, until the meat is very tender. Discard the bone. Season with salt, to taste.

Note: 'Vindaloo' is Portuguese for 'vinegar and garlic'. The clear vinegar is made from coconut, the dark from molasses, but white and balsamic vinegars can be used instead.

PANANG BEEF

SERVES 4–6

PASTE

8–10 large dried red chillies

6 red Asian shallots, chopped

6 garlic cloves, chopped

1 teaspoon ground coriander

1 tablespoon ground cumin

1 teaspoon white pepper

2 stems lemon grass, white part only, bruised and sliced

1 tablespoon chopped galangal

6 coriander (cilantro) roots

2 teaspoons shrimp paste

2 tablespoons toasted peanuts

1 tablespoon peanut oil

400 ml (14 fl oz) tin coconut cream

1 kg (2 lb 4 oz) round or blade steak, cut into 1 cm (½ inch) slices

400 ml (14 fl oz) tin coconut milk

4 tablespoons crunchy peanut butter

4 makrut (kaffir) lime leaves

3 tablespoons lime juice

2½ tablespoons fish sauce

3–4 tablespoons grated palm sugar or soft brown sugar

1 tablespoon chopped toasted peanuts, extra, to garnish

Thai basil, to garnish

1 To make the paste, soak the chillies in a bowl of boiling water for 15 minutes, or until soft. Remove the seeds and chop. Place in a food processor with the shallots, garlic, ground coriander, ground cumin, white pepper, lemon grass, galangal, coriander roots, shrimp paste and peanuts and process until smooth—add a little water if the paste is too thick.

2 Place the peanut oil and the thick coconut cream from the top of the can (reserve the rest) in a saucepan and cook over medium heat for 10 minutes, or until the oil separates. Add 6–8 tablespoons of the paste and cook, stirring, for about 6 minutes, or until fragrant.

3 Add the beef, coconut milk, peanut butter, lime leaves and the reserved coconut cream. Cook for 8 minutes, or until the beef just starts to change colour. Reduce the heat and simmer for 1 hour, or until the beef is tender.

4 Stir in the lime juice, fish sauce and sugar. Serve garnished with the peanuts and Thai basil.

TAMARIND BEEF

SERVES 4

2 tablespoons oil

1 kg (2 lb 4 oz) chuck steak, cut into 4 cm (1½ inch) cubes

2 red onions, sliced

3 garlic cloves, finely chopped

1 tablespoon julienned ginger

2 teaspoons ground coriander

2 teaspoons ground cumin

½ teaspoon ground fenugreek

½ teaspoon chilli powder

½ teaspoon ground cloves

1 cinnamon stick

125 g (4½ oz/½ cup) tamarind purée

6 curry leaves

250 ml (9 fl oz/1 cup) coconut cream

100 g (3½ oz) green beans, halved

fresh coriander (cilantro) sprigs, to garnish

1 **Heat the oil** in a large saucepan, add the beef in batches and cook over high heat for 2–3 minutes, or until browned. Remove.

2 **Add the onion** and cook over medium heat for 3 minutes, or until soft, then add the garlic and ginger, and cook for a further 2 minutes.

3 **Add the coriander**, cumin, fenugreek, chilli powder, cloves and cinnamon stick, and cook for 2 minutes.

4 **Return meat** to the pan and stir to coat with the spices. Add tamarind purée, curry leaves and 375 ml (13 fl oz/1½ cups) water. Bring to the boil, then reduce heat and simmer, covered, for 1½ hours, or until the beef is tender. Add coconut cream and cook, uncovered, for a further 10 minutes, then add the beans and cook for 5 minutes, or until tender but still crisp. Garnish with the coriander srigs and serve with rice.

BOMBAY LAMB CURRY

SERVES 4–6

1.5 kg (3 lb 5 oz) leg lamb, boned (ask your butcher to do this)
2 tablespoons ghee or oil
2 onions, finely chopped
2 garlic cloves, crushed
2 small green chillies, finely chopped
5 cm (2 inch) piece ginger, grated
1½ teaspoons ground turmeric
2 teaspoons ground cumin
3 teaspoons ground coriander
½–1 teaspoon chilli powder
1–1½ teaspoons salt
425 g (15 oz) tin crushed tomatoes
2 tablespoons coconut cream

1 Cut the meat into cubes, removing any skin and fat. You will have about 1 kg (2 lb 4 oz) meat remaining. Heat the ghee or oil in a large heavy-based frying pan (with a lid). Add the onion and cook, stirring frequently, over medium high heat for 10 minutes until golden brown. Add the garlic, chilli and ginger and stir for 2 minutes, taking care not to burn them.

2 Combine the spices and chilli powder in a small bowl. Stir to a smooth paste with 2 tablespoons water and add to the frying pan. Stir constantly for 2 minutes, taking care not to burn them.

3 Add the meat a handful at a time, stirring well to coat with spices—make sure all the meat is well-coated and browned.

4 Add salt to taste and stir in the tomato. Bring to the boil, cover and reduce the heat to low. Simmer for 45–60 minutes, until the lamb is tender. Stir in the coconut cream 30 minutes before the end of the cooking time.

Variation: Use 1 kg (2 lb 4 oz) beef, such as topside or round if preferred, and increase the cooking time to 1¼-1½ hours

SPICY GINGER AND BEEF CURRY

SERVES 4–6

1 kg (2 lb 4 oz) blade steak

2 tablespoons oil

2 garlic cloves, crushed

2 large onions, chopped

2 tablespoons finely grated ginger

1 small red chilli, finely chopped

1 teaspoon ground turmeric

1 teaspoon curry paste

1 small eggplant (aubergine), finely chopped

250 ml (9 fl oz/1 cup) coconut milk

185 ml (6 fl oz/¾ cup) beef stock

1 **Preheat the oven** to 160°C (315°F/Gas 2–3). Trim the meat of excess fat and sinew. Cut the meat evenly into 2.5 cm (1 inch) cubes.

2 **Heat the oil** in large heavy-based pan. Add the meat in small batches, cook over medium heat until well browned all over. Remove from the pan, drain on paper towels. Place in the casserole dish.

3 **Add the garlic**, onion, ginger, chilli, salt and pepper, turmeric and curry paste to the pan. Cook over low heat for 1 minute. Add eggplant, coconut milk and stock; simmer for 3 minutes. Carefully pour the curry sauce over the beef, cover. Bake for 1½ hours or until the beef is tender. Serve with rice.

CHICKEN AND VEGETABLE CURRY

SERVES 4

| 2 boneless, skinless chicken breast halves (about 175 g/6 oz) |
| 2 tablespoons oil |
| 4 tablespoons mild curry paste |
| 1 package (450 g/1 lb) frozen mixed Asian vegetables, thawed |
| 125 g (4½ oz/½ cup) plain yoghurt |

1   Rinse the chicken and pat dry with paper towels. Cut the chicken into 2 cm (¾ inch) cubes. Heat oil in a large frying pan

2   Add the chicken; cook over medium-high heat for about 4 minutes or until browned, stirring occasionally. Add the curry paste and vegetables to the pan; mix well.

3   Add 150 ml (5 fl oz/½ cup) water the pan. Bring to the boil, then reduce the heat to a simmer and cook, covered, for 3–5 minutes or until the vegetables and chicken are tender. Remove from the heat, stir in the yoghurt. Add salt to taste and serve immediately with hot, cooked rice.

Variation: Use fresh, chopped vegetables instead of frozen in this recipe.

FISH AND PEANUT CURRY

SERVES 6

4 tablespoons sesame seeds

½ teaspoon cayenne pepper

¼ teaspoon ground turmeric

1 tablespoon desiccated coconut

2 teaspoons ground coriander

½ teaspoon ground cumin

40 g (1½ oz/½ cup) crisp-fried onion (see Note)

5 cm (2 inch) piece ginger, chopped

2 garlic cloves, chopped

3 tablespoons tamarind purée

1 teaspoon salt

1 tablespoon crunchy peanut butter

1 tablespoon toasted peanuts

8 curry leaves, plus extra, to serve

1 kg (2 lb 4 oz) firm white fish fillets, skinless cut into 2 cm (¾ inch) cubes

1 tablespoon lemon juice

1 **Put the sesame seeds** in a heavy-based frying pan over medium heat and stir until golden. Add the cayenne pepper, turmeric, coconut, ground coriander and ground cumin and stir for a further minute, or until aromatic. Set aside to cool.

2 **Place fried onion,** ginger, garlic, tamarind, salt, peanut butter, toasted peanuts, sesame spice mix and 500 ml (17 fl oz/2 cups) hot water in a food processor and process until the mixture reaches a smooth, thick consistency.

3 **Put the sauce** and curry leaves into a heavy-based frying pan over medium heat and bring to a simmer. Cover and simmer over low heat for 15 minutes, then add the fish in a single layer. Simmer, covered, for a further 5 minutes, or until the fish is just cooked through. Gently stir through the lemon juice, and season well to taste. Garnish with curry leaves.

Note: To make crisp-fried onion at home, very thinly slice 1 onion, then dry on paper towel for 10 minutes. Fill a deep, heavy-based saucepan one-third full of oil and heat to 160°C (315°F), or until a cube of bread dropped into the oil browns in 30 seconds. Fry the onions for up to 1 minute, or until crisp and golden. Drain well, cool and store in an airtight container for up to 2 weeks. Use as a garnish and flavour enhancer for curries, rice and noodle dishes.

LAMB KORMA

SERVES 4

1 kg (2 lb 4 oz) lamb leg meat

2 onions, 1 chopped, 1 sliced

2 teaspoons grated ginger

4 garlic cloves

2 teaspoons ground coriander

2 teaspoons ground cumin

1 teaspoon cardamom seeds

¼ teaspoon cloves

¼ teaspoon ground cinnamon

3 long green chillies, seeded and chopped

2 tablespoons ghee or oil

2½ tablespoons tomato paste (concentrated purée)

125 g (4½ oz/½ cup) plain yoghurt

125 ml (4 fl oz/½ cup) coconut cream

50 g (1¾ oz/½ cup) ground almonds

toasted slivered almonds, to garnish

1 **Trim any excess fat** or sinew from the lamb, cut into 3 cm (1¼ in) cubes and put in a large bowl.

2 **Put the chopped onion,** ginger, garlic, coriander, cumin, cardamom seeds, cloves, cinnamon, chilli and ½ teaspoon salt in a food processor, or in a mortar with a pestle, and process or pound to a smooth paste. Add the spice paste to the lamb and mix well to coat. Leave to marinate for 1 hour.

3 **Heat the ghee** or oil in a large saucepan, add the sliced onion and cook, stirring, over low heat for 7 minutes, or until the onion is soft. Increase heat to medium–high and add lamb mixture and cook, stirring constantly, for about 8 minutes, or until the lamb changes colour.

4 **Stir in the tomato paste**, yoghurt, coconut cream and ground almonds. Reduce heat and simmer, covered, stirring occasionally, for about 1 hour, or until the meat is very tender. Add a little water if the mixture becomes too dry. Season well with salt and pepper. Serve garnished with slivered almonds.

BUTTER CHICKEN

SERVES 4–6

2 tablespoons peanut oil

1 kg (2 lb 4 oz) boneless, skinless chicken thighs, quartered

100 g (3½ oz) butter or ghee

3 teaspoons garam masala

2 teaspoons sweet paprika

1 tablespoon ground coriander

1 tablespoon finely chopped ginger

3 teaspoons ground cumin

2 garlic cloves, crushed

¼ teaspoon chilli powder

1 cinnamon stick

5 cardamom pods, bruised

2½ tablespoons tomato paste (concentrated purée)

1 tablespoon sugar

4 tablespoons plain yoghurt

185 ml (6 fl oz/¾ cup) cream

1 tablespoon lemon juice

1   **Heat a frying pan** or wok until very hot, add 1 tablespoon oil and swirl to coat. Add half the chicken thighs and stir-fry for 4 minutes, or until browned. Remove from the pan. Add extra oil, as needed, and cook the remaining chicken, then remove.

2   **Reduce the heat**, add the butter to the pan or wok and melt. Add the garam masala, sweet paprika, coriander, ginger, cumin, garlic, chilli powder, cinnamon stick and cardamom pods, and stir-fry for 1 minute, or until fragrant. Return the chicken to the pan and mix in the spices so it is well coated.

3   **Add the tomato paste** and sugar, and simmer, stirring, for 15 minutes, or until the chicken is tender and the sauce has thickened. Add the yoghurt, cream and lemon juice and simmer for 5 minutes, or until the sauce has thickened slightly.

BURMESE CHICKEN CURRY

SERVES 6

1 tablespoon medium-spiced Indian curry powder

1 teaspoon garam masala

½ teaspoon cayenne pepper

2 teaspoons sweet paprika

1.6 kg (3 lb 8 oz) chicken, cut into 8 pieces or 1.6 kg (3 lb 8 oz) mixed chicken pieces

2 onions, chopped

3 garlic cloves, crushed

2 teaspoons grated ginger

2 tomatoes, chopped

2 teaspoons tomato paste (concentrated purée)

1 stem lemon grass, white part only, thinly sliced

3 tablespoons oil

500 ml (17 fl oz/2 cups) chicken stock

½ teaspoon sugar

1 tablespoon fish sauce

1 Mix the curry powder, garam masala, cayenne pepper and paprika in a bowl. Rub this spice mix all over the chicken pieces and set aside.

2 Put the onion, garlic, ginger, tomato, tomato paste and lemon grass in a food processor, or in a mortar with a pestle, and process or pound to a smooth paste.

3 Heat oil in a large heavy-based frying pan (one that is large enough for the chicken to fit in a single layer) over medium heat, add the chicken and brown all over, then remove from the pan. In the same frying pan, add the onion paste and cook over low heat for 5–8 minutes stirring constantly. Return the chicken to the pan, and turn to coat in the paste.

4 Add the chicken stock and sugar and bring to a simmer. Reduce the heat to low, cover and cook for 1¼ hours, or until the chicken is very tender. While cooking, skim any oil that comes to the surface and discard. Stir in fish sauce and serve.

MUSAMAN BEEF CURRY

SERVES 4

1 tablespoon tamarind pulp

2 tablespoons oil

750 g (1 lb 10 oz) lean stewing beef, cubed

500 ml (17 fl oz/2 cups) coconut milk

4 cardamom pods, bruised

500 ml (17 fl oz/2 cups) coconut cream (do not shake the tins)

2–3 tablespoons musaman curry paste

8 baby onions

8 baby potatoes, cut in half if too large

2 tablespoons fish sauce

2 tablespoons shaved palm sugar (jaggery) or soft brown sugar

70 g (2½ oz/½ cup) unsalted toasted ground peanuts

coriander (cilantro) leaves, to serve

1 Put the tamarind pulp and 125 ml (4 fl oz/½ cup) boiling water in a bowl and set aside to cool. When cool, mash the pulp to dissolve in the water, then strain and reserve the liquid. Discard the pulp.

2 Heat the oil in a wok or a large saucepan and cook the beef in batches over high heat for 5 minutes, or until browned. Reduce the heat and add the coconut milk and cardamom, and simmer for 1 hour, or until the beef is tender. Remove the beef, strain and reserve the beef and cooking liquid.

3 Put the thick coconut cream from the top of the tins in a saucepan, bring to a rapid simmer over medium heat, stirring occasionally, and cook for 5–10 minutes, or until the mixture 'splits' (the oil starts to separate). Add the curry paste and cook for 5 minutes, or until it becomes aromatic.

4 Add the onions, potatoes, fish sauce, palm sugar, peanuts, beef, reserved cooking liquid and tamarind liquid, and simmer for 25–30 minutes. Garnish with fresh coriander leaves.

SERVES 6

1 tablespoon coriander seeds

2 teaspoons cumin seeds

1 teaspoon fennel seeds

1 tablespoon black peppercorns

3 tablespoons oil

1 kg (2 lb 4 oz) beef chuck, diced

2 onions, finely diced

4 garlic cloves, crushed

3 teaspoons finely grated ginger

1 red chilli, seeded, finely chopped

8 curry leaves

1 stem lemon grass, white part only, finely chopped

2 tablespoons lemon juice

250 ml (9 fl oz/1 cup) coconut milk

250 ml (9 fl oz/1 cup) beef stock

1 Dry-fry the coriander seeds, cumin seeds, fennel seeds, and black peppercorns in a frying pan over medium–high heat for 2–3 minutes, or until fragrant. Allow to cool. Using a mortar with a pestle, or a spice grinder, crush or grind to a powder.

2 Heat the oil in a heavy-based saucepan over high heat, brown the beef in batches, and set aside. Reduce the heat to medium, add the onion, garlic, ginger, chilli, curry leaves and lemon grass, and cook for 5–6 minutes, or until softened. Add the ground spices and cook for a further 3 minutes.

3 Return the beef to the pan, and stir well to coat with the spices. Add lemon juice, coconut milk and beef stock and bring to the boil. Reduce heat to low. Cook, covered, for about 2½ hours, or until beef is very tender and the sauce reduced. Skim off any oil that comes to the surface while cooking.

LAMB DHANSAK

SERVES 6

100 g (3½ oz/½ cup) yellow lentils

2 teaspoons dried yellow mung beans

2 tablespoons dried chickpeas

3 tablespoons red lentils

1 eggplant (aubergine), unpeeled

150 g (5½ oz) pumpkin (winter squash), unpeeled

2 tablespoons ghee or oil

1 onion, finely chopped

3 garlic cloves, crushed

1 tablespoon grated ginger

1 kg (2 lb 4 oz) boneless leg or shoulder of lamb, cut into 3 cm (1¼ inch) cubes

1 cinnamon stick

5 cardamom pods, bruised

3 cloves

1 tablespoon ground coriander

1 teaspoon ground turmeric

1 teaspoon chilli powder, or to taste

150 g (5½ oz) amaranth or English spinach leaves, cut into 5 cm (2 inch) lengths

2 tomatoes, halved

2 long green chillies, split lengthways, seeded

3 tablespoons lime juice

1   Soak the yellow lentils, yellow mung beans and chickpeas in water for about 2 hours, then drain well.

2   Put all four types of pulse in a saucepan, add 1 litre (35 fl oz/4 cups) water, cover and bring to the boil. Uncover and simmer for 15 minutes, skimming off any scum that forms on the surface, and stirring occasionally to make sure all the pulses are cooking at the same rate and are soft. Drain the pulses and lightly mash to a similar texture.

3   Cook the eggplant and pumpkin in boiling water for 10–15 minutes, or until soft. Scoop out the pumpkin flesh and cut it into pieces. Peel the eggplant carefully (it may be very pulpy) and cut the flesh into small pieces.

4   Heat the ghee or oil in a casserole dish or karahi (see note opposite) and fry the onion, garlic and ginger for 5 minutes, or until lightly brown and softened. Add the lamb and brown for

10 minutes, or until aromatic. Add the cinnamon, cardamom pods, cloves, coriander, turmeric and chilli powder and fry for 5 minutes to allow the flavours to develop. Add 170 ml (5½ fl oz/⅔ cup) water, cover and simmer for 40 minutes, or until the lamb is tender.

5   Add the mashed lentils and all the cooked and raw vegetables and chillies to the pan. Add the lime juice and simmer for 15 minutes. (If the sauce is too thick, add a little water.) Stir well, then check the seasoning. The dhansak should be flavoursome, aromatic, tart and spicy.

Note: A karahi is a deep, wok-shaped cooking dish used in Indian and Balti cooking. It lends itself perfectly to one-pot meals and can be taken straight from the stove to the table for serving.

MUSAMAN VEGETABLE CURRY

SERVES 4–6

MUSAMAN CURRY PASTE

1 tablespoon oil

1 teaspoon coriander seeds

1 teaspoon cumin seeds

8 cloves

½ teaspoon fennel seeds

4 cardamom seeds

6 red Asian shallots, chopped

3 garlic cloves, chopped

1 teaspoon finely chopped lemon grass

1 teaspoon finely chopped galangal

4 dried long red chillies

1 teaspoon ground nutmeg

1 teaspoon freshly ground white pepper

1 tablespoon oil

250 g (9 oz) baby onions

500 g (1 lb 2 oz) baby new potatoes

300 g (10 oz) carrots, roughly chopped

225 g (8 oz) tinned whole baby button mushrooms (champignons), drained

1 cinnamon stick

1 makrut (kaffir lime) leaf

1 bay leaf

coconut cream 250 ml (9 fl oz/1 cup)

1 tablespoon lime juice

3 teaspoons shaved palm sugar

1 tablespoon Thai basil, finely chopped

1 tablespoon roasted peanuts, crushed

1 Heat oil in a frying pan over low heat, add the coriander seeds, cumin seeds, cloves, fennel seeds and cardamom seeds, and cook for 1–2 minutes, or until fragrant.

2 Put the spices with the remaining curry paste ingredients in a food processor, or in a mortar with a pestle, and process or pound to a smooth paste. Add a little water if it is too thick.

3 Heat the oil in a large saucepan, add the curry paste and cook, stirring, over medium heat for 2 minutes, or until fragrant. Add the vegetables, cinnamon stick, makrut leaf, bay leaf and enough water to cover (about 500 ml/17 fl oz/2 cups), and bring to the boil. Reduce the heat and simmer, covered, stirring frequently, for 30–35 minutes, or until the vegetables are cooked.

4 Stir in the coconut cream and cook, uncovered, for 4 minutes, stirring frequently, until thickened slightly. Stir in the lime juice, palm sugar and chopped basil. Add a little water if the sauce is too dry. Top with the peanuts and extra basil leaves, to serve.

BEEF AND MUSTARD SEED CURRY

SERVES 6

3 tablespoons oil

2 tablespoons brown mustard seeds

4 dried red chillies

1 tablespoon yellow split peas

200 g (7 oz) French shallots, finely sliced

8 garlic cloves, crushed

1 tablespoons finely grated ginger

15 curry leaves

½ teaspoon ground turmeric

425 g (15 oz) tin tomatoes, chopped

1 kg (2 lb 4 oz) beef chuck, diced

435 ml (15¼ fl oz/1¾ cups) beef stock

1 Put the oil in a heavy-based saucepan over medium heat, add the mustard seeds, chillies and split peas. As soon as the mustard seeds start to pop, add the shallots, garlic, ginger, curry leaves and turmeric. Cook for 5 minutes, then add the tomatoes, beef and stock.

2 Bring to the boil then reduce to a simmer, cover and cook for 2 hours, or until the beef is very tender and the sauce reduced. While cooking, skim any oil that comes to the surface and discard.

PORK AND CARDAMOM CURRY

CURRY PASTE

10 cardamom pods
6 cm (2½ inch) piece ginger, chopped
3 garlic cloves, crushed
2 teaspoons black peppercorns
1 cinnamon stick
1 onion, finely sliced
1 teaspoon ground cumin
1 teaspoon ground coriander
1 teaspoon garam masala

3 tablespoons oil
1 kg (2 lb 4 oz) pork fillet, finely sliced
2 tomatoes, finely diced
125 ml (4 fl oz/½ cup) chicken stock
125 ml (4 fl oz/½ cup) coconut milk

1 **Lightly crush** the cardamom pods with the flat side of a heavy knife. Remove the seeds, discarding the pods. Put the seeds and the remaining curry paste ingredients in a food processor, or in a mortar with a pestle, and process or pound to a smooth paste.

2 **Put 2½ tablespoons** of oil in a large heavy-based frying pan, and fry the pork in batches until browned, then set aside. Add the remaining oil to the pan, then add the curry paste and cook over medium–high heat for 3–4 minutes, or until aromatic.

3 **Add the tomato,** chicken stock and coconut milk, and simmer covered over low–medium heat for 15 minutes. While cooking, skim any oil that comes to the surface and discard.

4 **Add the pork** to the sauce, and simmer uncovered for 5 minutes, or until cooked. Season well to taste and serve.

MALAYSIAN CHICKEN CURRY

SERVES 4–6

3 teaspoons dried shrimp

4 tablespoons oil

6–8 red chillies, seeded and finely chopped

4 garlic cloves, crushed

3 lemon grass stems, white part only, finely chopped

2 teaspoons ground turmeric

10 candlenuts

2 large onions, chopped

¼ teaspoon salt

250 ml (9 fl oz/1 cup) coconut milk

1.5 kg (3 lb 5 oz) chicken, cut into 8 pieces

125 ml (4 fl oz/½ cup) coconut cream

2 tablespoons lime juice

1 **Place the shrimp** in a frying pan and dry-fry over low heat, shaking the pan regularly, for 3 minutes, or until the shrimp are dark orange and are giving off a strong aroma. Allow to cool.

2 **Put the shrimp,** half the oil, chilli, garlic, lemon grass, turmeric and candlenuts in a food processor, or in a mortar with a pestle, and process or pound to a smooth paste.

3 **Heat the remaining** oil in a wok or frying pan, add the onion and salt, and cook, stirring regularly, over low–medium heat for 8 minutes, or until golden. Add the spice paste and stir for 5 minutes. If the mixture begins to stick to the bottom of the pan, add 2 tablespoons coconut milk. It is important to cook the mixture thoroughly as this develops the flavours.

4 **Add the chicken** to the wok or pan and cook, stirring, for 5 minutes, or until it begins to brown. Stir in the remaining coconut milk and 250 ml (9 fl oz/1 cup) water, and bring to the boil. Reduce the heat and simmer for 50 minutes, or until the chicken is cooked and the sauce has thickened slightly. Add the coconut cream and bring the mixture back to the boil, stirring constantly. Add the lime juice and serve immediately.

GOAN FISH CURRY

SERVES 6

3 tablespoons oil

1 large onion, finely chopped

4–5 garlic cloves, crushed

2 teaspoons grated ginger

4–6 dried red chillies

1 tablespoon coriander seeds

2 teaspoons cumin seeds

1 teaspoon ground turmeric

¼ teaspoon chilli powder

4 tablespoons desiccated coconut

270 ml (9½ fl oz) coconut milk

2 tomatoes, peeled and chopped

2 tablespoons tamarind purée

1 tablespoon white vinegar

6 curry leaves

1 kg (2 lb 4 oz) firm white fish fillets, skinless, cut into 8 cm (3 inch) pieces

1 **Heat the oil** in a large saucepan. Add the onion and cook, stirring, over a low heat for 10 minutes, or until softened and lightly golden. Add the garlic and ginger, and cook for a further 2 minutes.

2 **Dry-fry** the dried chillies, coriander seeds, cumin seeds, ground turmeric, chilli powder and desiccated coconut in a frying pan over medium–high heat for 2–3 minutes, or until fragrant. Allow to cool. Using a mortar with a pestle, or a spice grinder, crush or grind to a powder.

3 **Add the spice** mixture, coconut milk, tomato, tamarind, vinegar and curry leaves to the onion mixture. Stir to mix thoroughly, add 250 ml (9 fl oz/1 cup) water and simmer, stirring frequently, for 10 minutes, or until the tomato has softened and the mixture has thickened slightly.

4 **Add fish** and cook, covered, over low heat for 10 minutes, or until cooked through. Stir gently once or twice during the cooking and add a little water if the mixture is too thick.

SPICED CHICKEN WITH ALMONDS

SERVES 6

3 tablespoons oil

3 tablespoons slivered almonds

2 red onions, finely chopped

4–6 garlic cloves, crushed

1 tablespoon grated ginger

4 cardamom pods, bruised

4 cloves

1 teaspoon ground cumin

1 teaspoon ground coriander

1 teaspoon ground turmeric

½ teaspoon chilli powder

1 kg (2 lb 4 oz) boneless, skinless chicken thighs, trimmed

2 large tomatoes, peeled and chopped

1 cinnamon stick

100 g (3½ oz/1 cup) ground almonds

1 Heat 1 tablespoon oil in a large saucepan. Add almonds and cook over low heat for 15 seconds, or until lightly golden brown. Remove and drain on crumpled paper towel.

2 Heat the remaining oil, add the onion, and cook, stirring, for 8 minutes, or until golden brown. Add the garlic and ginger and cook, stirring, for 2 minutes, then stir in the spices. Reduce the heat to low and cook for 2 minutes, or until aromatic.

3 Add chicken and cook, stirring constantly, for 5 minutes, or until well coated with the spices and starting to colour.

4 Stir in the tomato, cinnamon stick, ground almonds and 250 ml (9 fl oz/1 cup) hot water. Simmer, covered, over low heat for 1 hour, or until the chicken is cooked through and tender. Stir often and add a little more water, if needed.

5 Leave the pan to stand, covered, for 30 minutes for the flavours to develop, then remove the cinnamon stick. Scatter the slivered almonds over the top and serve.

THAI GREEN CHICKEN CURRY

SERVES 4–6

GREEN CURRY PASTE

1 teaspoon white peppercorns
2 tablespoons coriander seeds
1 teaspoon cumin seeds
2 teaspoons shrimp paste
1 teaspoon sea salt
4 stems lemon grass, white part only, finely sliced
2 teaspoons chopped galangal
1 makrut (kaffir lime) leaf, shredded
1 tablespoon chopped coriander (cilantro) root
5 red Asian shallots, chopped
10 garlic cloves, crushed
16 long green chillies, seeded

500 ml (17 fl oz/2 cups) coconut cream (do not shake the tins)
2 tablespoons shaved palm sugar (jaggery)
2 tablespoons fish sauce
4 makrut (kaffir lime) leaves, shredded
1 kg (2 lb 4 oz) skinless, boneless chicken thighs or breasts, cut into thick strips
200 g (7 oz) bamboo shoots, cut into thick strips
100 g (3½ oz) snake (yard-long) beans, cut into 5 cm (2 inch) lengths
1 handful Thai basil

1 Dry-fry the peppercorns, coriander seeds, cumin seeds and shrimp paste wrapped in foil in a frying pan over medium–high heat for 2–3 minutes, or until fragrant. Allow to cool. Using a mortar with a pestle, or a spice grinder, crush or grind the peppercorns, coriander and cumin to a powder.

2 Put the shrimp paste and ground spices with the remaining curry paste ingredients in a food processor, or in a mortar with a pestle, and process or pound to a smooth paste.

3 Put the thick coconut cream from the top of the tins in a saucepan, bring to a rapid simmer over medium heat, stirring occasionally, and cook for 5–10 minutes, or until the mixture 'splits' (the oil starts to separate).

4 Add 4 tablespoons of the made green curry paste, then simmer for 15 minutes, or until fragrant. Add the palm sugar, fish sauce and makrut leaves to the pan.

5 Stir in the remaining coconut cream and the chicken, bamboo shoots and beans, and simmer for 15 minutes, or until the chicken is tender. Stir in the Thai basil and serve.

FISH KOFTAS IN TOMATO CURRY SAUCE

SERVES 6

KOFTAS

750 g (1 lb 10 oz) firm white fish fillets,
skinless, roughly chopped

1 onion, chopped

2–3 garlic cloves, crushed

1 tablespoon grated ginger

4 tablespoons chopped coriander
(cilantro) leaves

1 teaspoon garam masala

¼ teaspoon chilli powder

1 egg, lightly beaten

oil for shallow-frying

TOMATO CURRY SAUCE

2 tablespoons oil

1 large onion, finely chopped

3–4 garlic cloves, crushed

1 tablespoon grated ginger

1 teaspoon ground turmeric

1 teaspoon ground cumin

1 teaspoon ground coriander

1 teaspoon garam masala

¼ teaspoon chilli powder

800 g (1 lb 12 oz) tinned tomatoes,
crushed

3 tablespoons chopped coriander
(cilantro) leaves, plus extra sprigs,
to serve

1 Put the fish in a food processor, or in a mortar with a pestle, and process or pound to a smooth paste. Add the onion, garlic, ginger, coriander leaves, garam masala, chilli powder and egg, and process or pound until well combined. Using wetted hands, form 1 tablespoon of the mixture into a ball. Repeat with the remaining mixture.

2 To make the tomato curry sauce, heat the oil in a large saucepan, add onion, garlic and ginger, and cook, stirring often, over medium heat for 8 minutes, or until lightly golden.

3 Add the spices and cook, stirring, for 2 minutes, or until aromatic. Add the tomato and 250 ml (9 fl oz/1 cup) water, then reduce the heat and simmer, stirring frequently, for 15 minutes, or until reduced and thickened.

4 Heat the oil in a large frying pan to the depth of 2 cm (¾ inch). Add the fish koftas in three or four batches and cook for 3 minutes, or until browned all over. Drain on paper towel. Add the koftas to the sauce and simmer over low heat for 5 minutes, or until heated through. Gently fold in the coriander, season with salt and serve garnished with coriander sprigs.

PANEER AND PEA CURRY

SERVES 5

PANEER

2 litres (70 fl oz/8 cups) milk

4 tablespoons lemon juice

oil for deep-frying

CURRY PASTE

2 large onions

3 garlic cloves

1 teaspoon grated ginger

1 teaspoon cumin seeds

3 dried red chillies

1 teaspoon cardamom seeds

4 cloves

1 teaspoon fennel seeds

2 pieces cassia bark

500 g (1 lb 2 oz/3¼ cups) peas

2 tablespoons oil

400 ml (14 fl oz) tomato passata (puréed tomatoes)

1 tablespoon garam masala

1 teaspoon ground coriander

¼ teaspoon ground turmeric

1 tablespoon thick (double/heavy) cream

coriander (cilantro) leaves, to serve

1 Put the milk in a large saucepan, bring to the boil, stir in the lemon juice and turn off the heat. Stir the mixture for 1–2 seconds as it curdles. Put in a colander and leave for 30 minutes for the whey to drain off. Place the paneer curds on a clean, flat surface, cover with a plate, weigh down and leave for at least 4 hours.

2 Put all the curry paste ingredients in a food processor, or in a mortar with a pestle, and process or pound them to a smooth paste.

3 Cut the solid paneer into 2 cm (¾ inch) cubes. Fill a deep heavy-based saucepan one-third full of oil and heat to 180°C (350°F), or until a cube of bread browns in 15 seconds. Cook the paneer in batches for 2–3 minutes, or until golden. Drain on paper towel.

4 Bring a saucepan of water to the boil, add the peas and cook for 3 minutes, or until tender. Drain and set aside.

5 Heat the oil in a large saucepan, add the curry paste and cook over medium heat for 4 minutes, or until fragrant. Add the puréed tomato, spices, cream and 125 ml (4 fl oz/½ cup) water. Season with salt and simmer over medium heat for 5 minutes. Add the paneer and peas and cook for 3 minutes. Garnish with coriander leaves and serve.

FIVE-SPICE PORK CURRY

SERVES 4

500 g (1 lb 2 oz) pork spare ribs

1½ tablespoons oil

2 garlic cloves, crushed

190 g (6¾ oz) fried tofu puffs

1 tablespoon finely chopped ginger

1 teaspoon five-spice

½ teaspoon ground white pepper

3 tablespoons fish sauce

3 tablespoons kecap manis

2 tablespoons light soy sauce

3 tablespoons shaved palm sugar (jaggery)

1 small handful leaves coriander (cilantro), chopped thinly sliced

100 g (3½ oz) snow peas (mangetout), thinly sliced

1 Cut the spare ribs into 2.5 cm (1 inch) thick pieces, discarding any small pieces of bone. Put into a saucepan and cover with cold water. Bring to the boil then reduce to a simmer and cook for 5 minutes. Drain and set aside.

2 Heat the oil in a heavy-based saucepan over medium–high heat. Add pork and garlic and stir until lightly browned. Add the remaining ingredients except the snow peas, plus 560 ml (19 fl oz/2¼ cups) water. Cover, bring to the boil, then reduce to a simmer and cook, stirring occasionally, for about 15 minutes, or until the pork is tender. Stir in the snow peas.

LAMB AND SPINACH CURRY

SERVES 6

2 teaspoons coriander seeds

1½ teaspoons cumin seeds

3 tablespoons oil

1 kg (2 lb 4 oz) boneless leg or shoulder of lamb, cut into 2.5 cm (1 inch) cubes

4 onions, finely chopped

6 cloves

6 cardamom pods

1 cinnamon stick

10 black peppercorns

4 Indian bay (cassia) leaves

3 teaspoons garam masala

¼ teaspoon ground turmeric

1 teaspoon paprika

7.5 cm (3 inch) piece ginger, grated

4 garlic cloves, crushed

185 g (6½ oz/¾ cup) Greek-style yoghurt

450 g (1 lb) amaranth or English spinach leaves, roughly chopped

1 **Dry-fry the coriander** and cumin seeds in a frying pan over medium–high heat for 2–3 minutes, or until fragrant. Allow to cool. Using a mortar with a pestle, or a spice grinder, crush or grind to a powder.

2 **Heat the oil** in a flameproof casserole dish over low heat and fry a few pieces of meat at a time until browned. Remove from the dish. Add more oil to the dish, if necessary, and fry the onion, cloves, cardamom pods, cinnamon stick, peppercorns and bay leaves until the onion is lightly browned. Add the cumin and coriander, garam masala, turmeric and paprika and fry for 30 seconds.

3 **Add the meat**, ginger, garlic, yoghurt and 425 ml (15 fl oz) water and bring to the boil. Reduce the heat to a simmer, cover and cook for 1½–2 hours, or until the meat is very tender. At this stage, most of the water should have evaporated. If it hasn't, remove the lid, increase the heat and cook until the moisture has evaporated.

4 **Cook the spinach** briefly in a little simmering water until it is just wilted, then refresh in cold water. Drain thoroughly, then finely chop. Squeeze out any extra water in the spinach. Add the spinach to the lamb and cook for 3 minutes, or until the spinach and lamb are well mixed and any extra liquid has evaporated.

INDEX